For Tricia – my companion on

© Paul Kendall, 2023

All rights reserved. No part of this book may be reproduced in any form or by any electronic or mechanical means, including information storage and retrieval systems, without written permission from the author, except in the case of a reviewer, who may quote brief passages embodied in critical articles or in a review. Trademarked names appear throughout this book. Rather than use a trademark symbol with every occurrence of a trademarked name, names are used in an editorial fashion, with no intention of infringement of the respective owner's trademark. The information in this book is distributed on an "as is" basis, without warranty. Although every precaution has been taken in the preparation of this work, neither the author nor the publisher shall have any liability to any person or entity with respect to any loss or damage caused or alleged to be caused directly or indirectly by the information contained in this book.

UP, UP AND AWAY

April 22nd 2019

Tomorrow my wife Tricia and I will be embarking on a significant item from our bucket list – a coast-to-coast road trip across the United States. Starting in the Big Apple and, all being well, winding up six weeks later in San Francisco.

It's something I've dreamed of doing, ever since the teenage me was first captivated by all those hymns to American places and the thrill of the open road, and I first read about Jack Kerouac's travels and Woody Guthrie's life. Those songs and those books simply couldn't have been written about little old England. The roads aren't long enough and our national psyche isn't imbued with that restless pioneer spirit. "Take the last train to Clacton…"? "I was only 24 hours from Tewkesbury…"? "I left my heart in Sutton Coldfield…?" They don't have the same ring or conjure up the same fantasies, do they?

Tricia doesn't really recognise those fantasies. Her formative influences and cultural touchpoints have tended to be closer to home – The Beatles, The Famous Five and The Avengers (starring John Steed and Emma Peel, not a bunch of superheroes). But we do share a love of travel and she does like some of the music, so she's more than happy to come along for the ride.

This won't be our first visit to the States. Far from it. I had a few weeks in New York in the Spring of 1982, when I was working for what was, at the time, the world's biggest advertising agency. We've spent several family holidays emptying our bank account around the theme parks of Orlando, assisted by all or some of our four sons. I travelled the length of California and the breadth of Missouri with two of them, shooting a film in 2011. And Tricia and I reprised the Pacific Coast Highway bit of that expedition, from Los Angeles to Mendocino, when I went back to show the film in 2014. (It was a documentary called 'The Byrd Who Flew Alone', about Gene Clark, the great singer/songwriter and a founder member of The Byrds, America's answer to The Beatles. Google it, if you're interested in knowing more.)

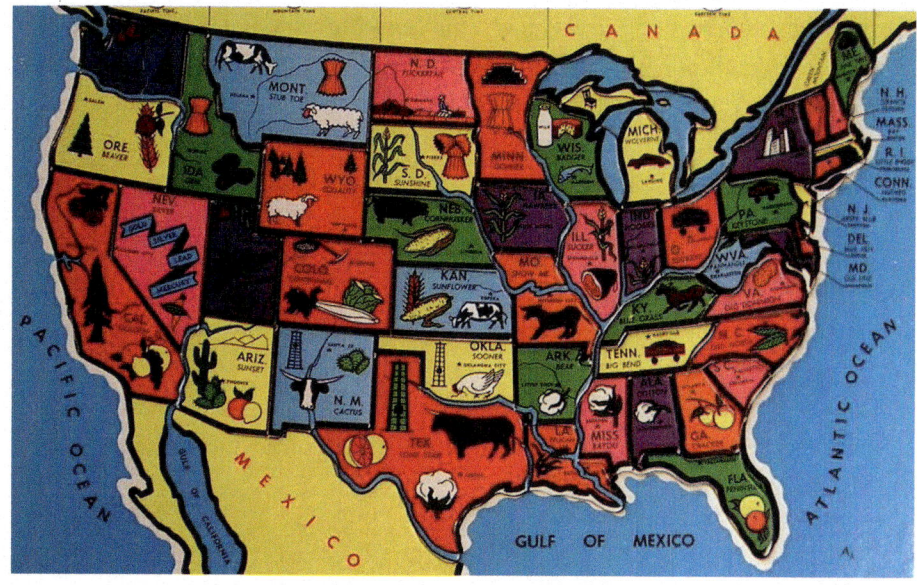

So many places… so little time.

The vast expanse between the two coasts is mostly unfamiliar territory, however. At least in terms of first-hand experience. And it's only in the last couple of years, since getting full control of our own work schedules, that we've been able to consider taking several weeks of time out in one go, to explore it without rushing. We had intended to do it in 2018, but a family event (a joyous one – the birth of our first grandson) meant it had to be postponed.

There are, of course, an infinite variety of ways to drive from the east coast of America to the west, on highways large and small. Any one of which would mean missing out on sights and memories, which might be deemed unmissable.

Our original idea, to give ourselves some structure, was to plot our journey using places with Ruby in their name, as we were celebrating our Ruby Wedding Anniversary that year. There are a fair few eligible locations scattered across the country, from remote lakes, waterfalls and mountain ranges to small communities and abandoned mining towns. Plus a myriad of cafes, bars and other retailers, most of them outlets of Ruby Tuesday.

We did a similar thing, on a much smaller scale, when we were in South Africa to mark our Pearl (30th) Anniversary. As part of that trip we visited Paarl, which is Afrikaans for 'pearl'. But that was an easy day trip from Cape Town; the drive through the mountains and wine regions of the Western Cape was utterly gorgeous; and Paarl had at least a couple of sights worth seeing – the expansive Afrikaans Language Monument and the vineyards.

On revisiting the road maps and guidebooks for our American venture, however, it became clear that pursuing the 'Ruby' line of thought in earnest would almost certainly involve lots of extra miles for what would probably be very little reward. The clue is in words such as 'remote' and 'abandoned'.

Visiting Ruby in South Carolina, for example, would require a deviation of 200 miles each way from our intended route through the Blue Ridge Mountains. It has a population of less than four hundred and, according to Trip Advisor, absolutely nothing to offer by way of accommodation, refreshment or things to do.

Ruby in Arizona, on the other hand, sounds like a well-preserved and atmospheric ghost town, home to a once productive mine and a series of gruesome homicides in the 1920s. But it's situated a mere four miles from the Mexican border (an even longer diversion from Plan A), over 4000ft up at the end of a twelve-mile dirt road. It's doubtful that our car hire company would approve.

I rest my case.

Not all Rubys are so inaccessible, it has to be said. Ruby's Inn & Restaurant in Purcell, Oklahoma, for example, is (or at least, was) not far off the journey we hope to make, along what we're assured is the most authentic remaining section of old Route 66, running between Tulsa and Amarillo. Reviews on Trip Advisor, however, suggested that going there would be a gamble. On the one hand, there are 5-star effusions, lauding it as "a gem" and "a great old-style diner". And on the other there's a 1-star submission, titled 'Crackheads', which bluntly states "This is the most discussing (sic) place I've ever been. The food is half cooked and the servers are all drug users." But I guess that may have been written by a rival establishment in town.

Far more enticing was Ruby's Horseback Rides, which take you on a tour of Bryce Canyon in Utah. On the face of it, this would definitely be worth doing. But as Tricia has become nervous of riding, even in the most placid surroundings, it seemed unlikely she would warm to the idea of doing it in this particular place. While Bryce Canyon looks to be one of Mother Nature's more spectacular upheavals, it's characterised by narrow trails, steep inclines and vertiginous drops.

Instead, the itinerary will revolve around musical pilgrimages, across a number of genres, and several chapters of 'The Most Scenic Drives In America' – a mouth-watering book, which I was given for Christmas and have been devouring ever since. And it will involve minimal use of freeways, wherever practical. Details will be revealed in the fullness of time.

There are a few fixed points established in advance – flights into New York and back from San Francisco; tickets for shows in Nashville and Las Vegas; and lodgings arranged at Monument Valley, the Grand Canyon and Yosemite, where options were already getting limited several months ahead. Apart from that we've tried to leave things open, as much as possible, to allow for spontaneity and changes of plan. For the most part we'll just book 24 hours ahead, when we have a better idea of where the next day will take us.

What follows is being done mainly as a memento/reminder for ourselves in our dotage. But if you'd like to find out where those musical pilgrimages take us and to see if our marriage survives six weeks of being in each other's pockets 24/7, you're most welcome to join us.

Song for the day: Lenny Kravitz – 'Fly Away'
There are a few obvious contenders for first ditty of the trip. 'Leaving On A Jet Plane' and 'Up Up And Away', to name but two. But, much as I admire Jimmy Webb's songwriting, they're both a bit sappy. Lenny does a much better job of capturing the anticipation we're feeling, as we prepare to set off.

Day 1 - QUICK, QUICK, SLOW.

London → New York

So here we are in the Big Apple, after a very long day of expectations exceeded and expectations disappointed.

Here we go, here we go, here we go.

We flew from Heathrow to Newark with United Airlines. A risky strategy, perhaps, given that United consistently score badly in customer satisfaction surveys, while their idea of "friendly skies" has involved assaulting a passenger and dragging him from his seat, to make way for an employee. They've also left a blind person behind on a plane, to be discovered by the maintenance crew; been involved in the misplacement and deaths of numerous animals; and refused boarding to girls wearing leggings. But, as we were confident that we'd be able-bodied, pet-free and suitably dressed, the price difference between them and other airlines was too wide to ignore. We were also able to book a civilised schedule, leaving London at 4pm and arriving at 7pm, Eastern Time, which would hopefully allow us to have dinner and get to bed at a sensible hour, if we ignore the four hours' time difference.

The gamble paid off, at least on the outward journey. (We've still got to get back!) We were sitting together with a window seat; the food bordered on tolerable; the in-flight entertainment offering was probably the best we've ever experienced; we arrived bang on time; and they managed to put our luggage on the same flight. All good so far.

Then we got off the plane.

We'd been told, by a very experienced traveller, that Newark is the best point of entry to New York by air, being smaller and less busy than JFK, and therefore quicker and easier to get through. Three hours later, we had to disagree. Passport control for non-US arrivals had some thirty desks available, of which only six were open when the population of our flight joined an already lengthy queue. Two of those were dedicated to folk in wheelchairs and their entourages, of which there seemed to be an extraordinary number. And two of the remaining four soon closed, as their occupants finished their shifts or took a break. For any younger readers, who've never needed to acquire the ability to do mental arithmetic, that left two desks to process everyone else.

When our turn came, after well over an hour of intermittent shuffling forwards, the officer dealing with us was unusually friendly for a Homeland Security representative. He did, however, need a geography lesson about the Isle of Sheppey – my birthplace – before being convinced that it wasn't on Trump's banned list. (It's a small island, near the mouth of the Thames Estuary in the south east of England, linked to the mainland by a couple of bridges. It's notably unlovely and a visit is not recommended. But the hospital in Minster had the closest maternity unit to my parents' home in Sittingbourne, Kent, when I put in my appearance. I'm told that my father followed the ambulance, which carried my mother, on his bicycle.)

On the plus side, I wasn't seized and held in a side office for a couple of hours, which is what happened when we went to Florida with our two younger sons, back in 2007. Terrorist attacks in Glasgow and London, a few days before, had triggered a heightened state of alert, and the immigration guys been instructed to pay special attention to all males aged between 18 and 45, regardless of ethnicity or country of origin or any suspicious circumstances. As I was 54 at the time, I should probably have felt flattered to be included. But Jack, who had recently celebrated his 21st birthday, was blithely ignored. Which suggested that passports weren't being scrutinised too carefully. My 'interview', when it finally started, took all of ninety seconds, most of which were taken up with profuse apologies, as the official allocated to me realised the mistake.

Once through the formalities in Newark it should have been plain sailing, thanks to our pre-booked tickets for the 'skip the lines' Super Shuttle, which would deliver us direct to our hotel. Sadly the service seemed to be characterised by incompetence, lethargy and disinformation. We'll spare you the tedious details. Just be wary of anything calling itself 'super' in future. Over 90 more minutes elapsed before we were finally heading out of the airport and across the Hudson River, in a minibus laden with equally disgruntled passengers.

We were, of course, the last people to be dropped off, but at least we got a bonus tour of Manhattan after dark. Most of it was surprisingly quiet, for the city that never sleeps. There was no sign of hamburgers sizzling on an open grill, let alone jukeboxes jumping with records and, unlike Chuck Berry, being back in the USA wasn't making us feel so good today. We're sure things will look very different after a decent night's sleep.

Our hotel, by the way, is unexceptional, even at $250 per night. The bed is small for a double, especially given the size of the average American, and the modest proportions of the room mean it has to be used for opening suitcases. We are, however, brilliantly located, within minutes of

Broadway, the Empire State Building and Macy's, and just a short stroll from Central Park. Which is where we'll be headed, once we're fully awake and refreshed.

Song for the day: Art Garfunkel – 'A Heart In New York'
Many songs have been written about the Big Apple, but this one is unbeatably appropriate for the occasion – "New York, to that tall skyline I come, Flying in from London to your door". It was written and originally recorded by a couple of Scots, Gallagher & Lyle, but this version obviously has an even closer association with the city. It was a highlight of Simon & Garfunkel's concert in Central Park in 1981.

Day 2 - WHAT A DIFFERENCE A DAY MAKES

New York

A glorious Spring day in Manhattan was put to full use - as the 30,000 steps recorded by my 'activity tracker' testify.

You know you're in New York when you've barely left your hotel and, at the end of the street, blue lights and sirens are descending from all directions. The cross section was taped off, a swarm of New York's finest were busy keeping traffic and pedestrians at bay, and I counted at least six patrol cars, three fire engines and an ambulance. More were arriving when we were told that the 'situation' was just a manhole fire. "Nothing to see here", indeed.

You also know you're in New York when an elderly woman is wandering around, wearing only stars'n'stripes knickers, a blonde wig and a cowboy hat, with a guitar inscribed 'The naked cowgirl' covering her sagging breasts, and no-one – apart from Japanese tourists capturing the moment for posterity – bats an eyelid.

In Easter week the town was busy, even by New York standards. Going up 5th Avenue at the start of the day and down Broadway at the end required careful navigation through the madding crowd and a patience that isn't usually my strong suit. But the place looked stunning. The gold on the statue at the Rockefeller Center skating rink and on Trump Tower glistened; the taller buildings reflected the blue skies and each other; and Central Park was in magnificent bloom.

The park was hectic, of course, though spacious enough not to feel overstuffed. We even managed to get an outside table at The Tavern On The Green – the ideal spot for a light lunch and a bit of people watching. Over the next hour, a complete cross-section of New Yorkers passed us by – from expensively-suited execs braying into their phones to homeless guys delving into waste bins; from couples of all ages, ambling arm in arm, to joggers and roller skaters of all ages, in earnest pursuit of eternal youth; and from nannies chaperoning the next generation of Masters of the Universe to buskers looking to earn the next meal.

The scene of the crime(s).

When we reluctantly dragged ourselves away from our place in the sun, the first musical pilgrimage of the trip took us to Strawberry Fields, the homage to John Lennon a little further up the west side of the park. This one was probably more for Tricia. As children of the sixties, The Beatles have figured prominently in the soundtrack of both our lives, but they've always been particularly special to her. They were her first girlhood crush and Paul remained her dream man, right up until her tastes matured and she belatedly fell for Leonard Cohen, after seeing him in concert in 2008. She also reckons she'd bumped into the fab foursome at a Middlesbrough bus stop, when she was about nine years old, which cemented them in her affections. (I've always been suspicious of this claim, but The Beatles did indeed play a Middlesbrough gig in 1963, so maybe she did.)

We'd seen the real, singular Strawberry Field on a visit to Liverpool, a few years earlier, as part of a National Trust tour of Beatles landmarks. The boyhood homes of John and Paul were included in the itinerary, and the tour was the only way you could see inside them. While we were at the McCartney house a busload of Japanese tourists arrived outside. They couldn't get in, so had to content themselves with many photos of the outside and a glimpse of the man who looked after the place, peeping through the net curtains. He looked remarkably like the ageing Paul, to the point where we initially wondered if he might be a relative (he wasn't). When the Japanese folk spotted him, they jumped to the wrong conclusion and went crazy.

The real Strawberry Field - before it was tarted up as a tourist attraction, complete with exhibits, gift shop and café – was an overgrown, untended piece of urban wilderness behind padlocked, rusting iron gates. The Gothic mansion in the grounds had been demolished in 1973, but an eerie, melancholy feel hung over the place on the misty day that we were there. It was perfect for the occasion.

The New York version may have added an 's' to the name, in keeping with the song, but it's subtracted from the atmosphere and was sadly unimpressive. Yoko has reportedly contributed a million dollars to the establishment and maintenance of her husband's memorial. We struggled to see how that money has been spent.

Apart from the little signs at either end of the short walk through one of the less attractive (and, by the look of it, less cared for) sections of the park, the only thing to identify its significance was the Imagine Mosaic - a small and unremarkable example of the art. Even that had started sinking into the ground a few years earlier, becoming lopsided and cracked, due to inadequate foundations, and needed to be restored. Oh… there was also a middle-aged man, sitting on a nearby bench, warbling 'Imagine' to the accompaniment of an out-of-tune guitar. I would happily have given him money to cease and desist, but others seemed to be rewarding his efforts, so I doubt that would have worked.

The Dakota Building, directly across the street from the park, was far more affecting. All was quiet and there were absolutely no reminders of the tragic event that it had witnessed. The days when the entrance was piled high with flowers and other tributes, and the street was crowded with mourners and media, are long gone. The liveried doorman cheerily pointed out where Lennon had been shot and fallen, and we stood for a few moments in respectful memory of what the world had lost that night in December 1980. Then we took some selfies.

Strawberry Fields – but maybe not forever.

Our original plan, of starting our New York experience with a visit to the Top of the Rock observation deck, was foiled by the afore-mentioned crowds. Every single time slot had been taken before the day even started, as was the case for each day of our stay. But our other ambition, to score some cheap tickets for a Broadway show, was more successful.

When we first passed the TKTS outlet on Times Square, in the middle of the afternoon, the queue was very long. Having had our fill of waiting in line, while at Newark Airport, we passed it by. But a couple of hours later it had shrunk significantly and within ten minutes we were the delighted holders of tickets for 'Jersey Boys' at a fraction of the usual price.

With enough time for our first proper meal of the trip, ahead of the show starting, we decided to dive in at the deep end of dining US-style and succumbed to the lure of a nearby establishment inviting us to 'Try Our Famous BBQ Pulled Pork Sliders'.

We're no strangers to the ways of our cousins on this side of the Atlantic and their concept of what constitutes a portion. But what we got was a sharp reminder of the peril to waistlines and cholesterol levels, that the coming weeks will present. The sliders, which we'd naively imagined as being quite petite, turned out to be roughly the size of a McDonalds burger, only filled to overflowing with meat and oozing sauce in every direction. Two or three, at the most, would have made a more than adequate meal. We were each presented with six, accompanied by a small bucket of fries and a mountain of salad, plus an array of condiments.

We were hungry, the food was good and we did our best, but we had to give up the struggle with our plates only half emptied. Our waitress was most concerned that we weren't happy with what we'd been given. The idea that we couldn't, or wouldn't, force it all down was clearly alien to her. Her confusion was only compounded when, not wishing to inflict pungent aromas on the theatre or our hotel room, and being reluctant to see a slider again for at least a month, we spurned the offer of doggy bags. Effusive compliments and thanks were required, before she was able to relax. We imagined her telling her incredulous colleagues about the weird Brits who hardly ate anything, after we'd left.

Feeling like Mr Creosote, from Monty Python's 'Meaning Of Life', we staggered the short distance to the theatre and slumped in our seats, semi-prone and unmoving, trying to breathe normally, for long enough to regain some semblance of comfort before the curtain rose.

The show, based on the story and songs of Frankie Valli & The Four Seasons, was every bit as good as when we saw it in London, imaginatively staged and performed with terrific energy, enthusiasm and talent. All buoyed up by an audience that was the vocal and unrestrained epitome of what you'd expect an American crowd to be. There's no doubt that musical theatre, like comedy and sport, is hugely enhanced by sharing it with a large congregation of like-minded others.

The evening ended with a leisurely stroll through the sights and sounds of Times Square, back to our hotel. You can't help suspecting that half the people there are eying you up as a potential mark, but that tension is part of what makes the city so stimulating. The perfect end to what had been, in its way, a perfect New York day.

Song for the day: Lou Reed – 'Perfect Day'
The ideal fit for the occasion, from New York's premier rock'n'roll poet. OK, so I know it's allegedly an homage to heroin addiction, and was used as such in 'Trainspotting'. But Lou has adamantly denied that interpretation (as you might expect) and the song has been covered in contexts that are far more innocent. As so often, the original version is the best.

Day 3 - FREE AT LAST!

New York

It's ironic that, in a city which is one of the great centres of capitalism and often seems intent on emptying your pockets as ruthlessly and efficiently as possible, some of the most iconic and memorable attractions don't cost a dime. Central Park is an obvious one and today we sampled three more.

The High Line is a brilliant idea and a fine example of what collective effort can achieve at community level. A long disused railway track, running for about a mile and a half through the old Meatpacking District on the western side of the city, has been turned into an elevated urban walking trail, embellished with plant life and artworks. It offers expansive views across the Hudson to New Jersey (whose skyline is starting to mimic Manhattan's these days), and down to the Statue of Liberty and Ellis Island.

It's undoubtedly been successful in drawing visitors - and therefore commerce - to an area which was being left to die. But there have been victims of that success, as illustrated by the excellent 'Class Divide' documentary (available to view on YouTube, the last time I looked).

On my one previous visit to New York, in 1982, the Meatpacking District was among several areas of Manhattan that were effectively no-go zones, as the city teetered on the brink of bankruptcy and chaos. In the mornings it was still home to bustling meat markets, as the name suggests, but for the rest of the day it was mostly handed over to hookers, drug dealers, gay nightlife and hardcore sex clubs.

Eventually the remnants of the meat trade moved to the Bronx, with the opening of a new warehouse in 2002, and there was a brief period when low rents attracted something of an artistic community. But then developers took over. The old buildings that used to sit alongside the track are being replaced by flash apartment blocks and offices, swiftly followed by swanky bars, restaurants and boutiques, and it's now one of the most expensive neighbourhoods in the city. Local residents are being priced out and many stretches of the High Line currently feel more like a walkway through a building site.

Living the High Line.

Something that doesn't seem to have changed much through the years is the Staten Island Ferry. The venerable old boats exist, first and foremost, as an admirably public-spirited commuter service, run without charge, for the only one of the five boroughs that doesn't have bridge or tunnel links to Manhattan. They also provide a great sightseeing opportunity. Which is why it was rush hour on board, even when it wasn't rush hour.

A day, that was already in chilly contrast to yesterday's sun-drenched idyll, turned positively Arctic as we left the relative shelter of the dockside. Nevertheless we gritted our teeth and went on deck, to get better views of the Statue of Liberty and Ellis Island, where arrivals from the old world in the first half of the 20th century were processed, before being allowed to start their new lives in the land of opportunity.

From what we've already seen on the streets of New York, and what we know about the increasing levels of poverty, wildly unbalanced wealth distribution and breakdown of social services in the United States, there's a hollow ring these days to the words most commonly associated with the Statue of Liberty – "Give me your tired, your poor, Your huddled masses yearning to breathe free…". 21st century America has her own surfeit of such wretched souls and Agent Orange is doing his best not to let any more in. It was a fine sentiment while it lasted, though, and one can only imagine how a first view of the statue felt, to those who were investing so much hope in what it represented.

A distant dream

Most of our fellow passengers on the ferry went straight back, when we reached the other side. But we felt we should at least have a quick look at Staten Island, on what might well be our only ever visit, so we wandered away from the terminal in search of refreshment. After half an hour of battling the elements along dreary, windswept streets, we'd almost given up hope when we stumbled across Bella Giornata, a characterful and amiable luncheonette, offering excellent sandwiches and a welcome that suggested they didn't get too many Brits dropping in. It turned out it was only five minutes' walk from the ferry, if we'd gone up the hill in a straight line. And it's recommended, should you ever find yourself on Staten Island.

A route through Battery Park, on our return to Manhattan, took us past the cruise boats which are the other way of getting close to Lady Liberty. Our smugness re the queues avoided and the money saved will hopefully be excused.

And so at last to Ground Zero, or The World Trade Center Site as it's now called. The day had been getting progressively colder and darker, after a bright start. Just as we reached the two huge holes in the ground, where the twin towers had stood, a steady rain began to fall. It seemed appropriate. It also drove away the handful of other sightseers, leaving us in eerie isolation. A far cry from the scenes of panic and pandemonium, which we've come to associate with this place.

9/11 is one of those occasions, like the Kennedy assassination, when people can pinpoint exactly what they were doing as the news hit. I was 10, on November 22nd 1963. Our family didn't have a TV at the time, but the old lady next door did and she was always happy to have some company. So that's where I was. I've absolutely no idea what we were watching, but I can remember the sombre newsflash that interrupted the programming. I raced home, in high excitement, to share the information. I had minimal understanding of the event's importance, at the time, but my father's shock and my mother's tears have always stayed with me.

Fast forward to September 2001. It was lunchtime and I was almost the only person around in the creative department of the London advertising agency, where I worked. (This was right at the end of the Mad Men era, when advertising lunches were invariably still liquid and often lasted all afternoon. I would usually have been found in a nearby hostelry, with the rest of the department.) A TV was on in the creative director's glass-fronted office and my attention was caught by what looked like some kind of dramatic explosion in New York.

As I went in to see what was going on, the commentary over the live footage of a burning World Trade Center tower was saying that the cause of the explosion was unknown. At that very moment, the second plane went into the second tower, and it was instantly apparent that this was no coincidence.

The office filled up over the next hour, as word spread and people came in to watch developments. On the news, a succession of correspondents and experts offered informed opinion and guesswork, while the towers continued to burn on a large screen in the background. The most surreal moment came when, with the talking heads gabbing on, oblivious to what was happening behind them, the first tower collapsed in what felt like slow motion, leaving the in-studio screen filled with smoke and dust. A gasp of horror and disbelief went round the room. I think we all instinctively knew that we'd just seen a turning point in world history.

Returning to 2019, by the time we'd finished contemplating the austere reflecting pools, which occupy the footprints of the twin towers, we were ready for bodies and spirits to be warmed in equal measure. Although we're primarily country people at heart, a real advantage to being in a big city (one that I'm sure we'll come to miss, when we're out in the sticks) is a wealth of options for finding sustenance. Nowhere is this more true than in New York City, where every imaginable cuisine and ambience is usually within a stone's throw of wherever you happen to be.

Having enjoyed an al fresco experience in the Central Park sunshine yesterday, today's very different conditions demanded something from the opposite end of the spectrum. Comfort food in cosy surroundings was required, and we found both in a classic old school trattoria, just off Broadway. Most of our fellow diners could have been auditioning for bit parts in The Sopranos, by the look of them. But, so long as no-one came out of the restroom packing heat and spraying bullets, their presence – along with a menu that read like an Antonio Carluccio recipe book - gave us confidence that the service would be solicitous and the cooking of a high standard. Which they were.

Song for the day: Bruce Springsteen – My City Of Ruins
This was written in the aftermath of 9/11, but could apply to all too many communities across the USA, brought low by changes that were probably beyond their control and failures or false priorities that weren't. New York, for all its ongoing issues, is in a far better state than when I was last here. Hopefully other places will be able to find the same upward trajectory.

Day 4 - WET, WET, WET

New York

New York is notorious for its changeable climate. As has just been demonstrated. On my previous visit, which lasted a little over a month, every meteorological event, from blizzards to heatwaves, had passed through. This much shorter stay was to be no different. After basking in sunshine on Wednesday, today the rain came down in earnest and the wind blasted along the avenues. Guys touting umbrellas of unproven quality materialised at every subway entrance, and crossing any street involved trying to find a way round rapidly expanding lakes. At one point we were stuck indoors for the best part of an hour, while monsoon-like conditions raged outside. (The doors in question belonged to a very nice coffee shop, so it could have been worse.)

Even more unfortunately, it was the day we were due to take two walking tours of the Greenwich Village area – a daytime one, around landmarks of note, and an evening Ghost Tour. A visit to the Met or the Frick might have been a better option, with hindsight. But, as the no-nonsense Nu Joysey lady leading the first tour said "Youse guys is from Engerland, roit? Youse is used to a bit a rain." So we toughed it out.

Both tours were run by Free Tours By Foot – a concept that we first encountered on our trip to Australia in 2017. It now seems to have spread worldwide. There are few major cities where a range of 'free' walking tours aren't available. The principle is that, rather than paying an exorbitant fee up front and hoping for the best, you give the guide what you think the tour was worth, when it ends.

The upside of this approach is that you're in control of the cost and the guides should theoretically be motivated to give it their all, every time. The downside, for the guides, is that they're entirely reliant on their customers playing the game. Which, all too often, they don't. On every such tour we've taken, here and in Australia, a significant proportion of the group snuck away without giving anything. Shame on them, I say. One can only trust that the Law of Karma will make them pay for their dishonourable stinginess.

Treading damply in the footsteps of greatness.

The days when the Village was a vibrant hub of creativity, drawing musicians, writers and artists from far and wide, are long gone. Cheap rents are a thing of the distant past, as are most of the iconic venues. The folk who live there now are those who can afford to pay many millions of dollars for a modestly sized home (eg Robert de Niro, whose townhouse looks out over the swimming pool used in 'Raging Bull') or the $70k a year fees at NYU, which has completely monopolised the surrounds of Washington Square Park.

As with Sunset Strip in LA, it's been turned over to tourists like us and the real action has moved elsewhere… out to Williamsburg in Brooklyn, in this case. The Minetta Tavern – the watering hole that once had the likes of Hemingway, Dylan Thomas and Ezra Pound propping up the bar – has kept its scruffy exterior, but inside is an upmarket restaurant. As the maître d' made very clear, when we tried to go in, just following in legendary footsteps for a quick drink is not the order of the day. Right across the street Cafe Wha, where an unknown Robert Zimmerman first attracted attention and Chas Chandler discovered Jimi Hendrix, is one of the last original music places still standing. Other echoes of a colourful past linger, however, and were conjured up by our daytime tour.

The Stonewall Inn, on Christopher Street, can justifiably claim to be the start point of the gay liberation movement. The Stonewall Riots, in June 1969, were the first high profile example of the gay community fighting back against discrimination and harassment, and became a trigger for the wave of activism that followed. The Inn and the surrounding streets have been designated as a national monument, in recognition of this significance, and a statue of four figures (two men and two women) in the neighbouring park marks the spot. The Stonewall and Christopher Street continue to be an epicentre of LGBT life in the city.

A building offering less historic resonance, but prompting far greater interest among our tour group, stood on a quiet corner a few blocks away. It didn't look anything special, but we were informed (or rather, I was informed… everyone else seemed to recognise it right away) that it was used as the exterior of the apartment inhabited by an assortment of 'Friends'. A restaurant occupied the ground floor beneath it and was the cause of some disappointment among the assembled company. To be true to the TV series, it should have been a coffee shop called Central Perk, apparently. I didn't bother to point out that 'Friends' is fictional, and that locations are cut and pasted, or recreated, all the time in film making. On Googling the matter, back at the hotel, I discovered that the show was actually shot in a Hollywood studio, and none of the cast were filmed anywhere near New York.

Far more impressive, from both architectural and narrative standpoints, was the Jefferson Market Courthouse, an elaborate Gothic pile on 6th Avenue. It's a library now, but originally it was, as the name suggests, a place where justice was administered. It hosted some notable trials in its day, including the infamous Mae West obscenity case in 1927. Ms West had written, directed and acted in a Broadway play called (perhaps ill-advisedly) 'Sex'. It helped make her one of the most glittering stars of the time and, for a while, the second highest paid person in the country, after newspaper tycoon William Randolph Hearst. It also saw her fined $500 and sentenced to 10 days in jail. She was released early due to good behavior, prompting the archetypal Mae West quip: "It's the first time I ever got anything for good behavior". Our guide took great delight in sharing that tale with us.

In the break between tours, we went for an early dinner at what *Time Out* reckons is the best place to eat on MacDougal Street – once the spiritual heart of bohemian Greenwich Village, with former residents ranging from Louisa May Alcott to His Bobness. The reputation of La Lanterna di Vittorio was confirmed by its evident popularity, and we counted ourselves very lucky to get a table by the window overlooking the street. Five minutes later, folk were being turned away.

Fortified by excellent pizzas, coffee and beer, we were ready to embark on the evening Ghost Tour. To be perfectly honest, though, it was probably a walk too far. From the get-go, our guide seemed to be put out of spirits (if you'll excuse the play on words) by the miserable weather and its inevitable effect on the size of the group (just six hardy souls, including ourselves). Whatever the reason, the presentation had little of the flair that made previous such tours so enjoyable, and we got the impression she would have been happy to abandon proceedings at the earliest opportunity. She was not alone.

We were led round a trail of places with supposedly supernatural connections, none of which stood out as being especially unusual or credible. The two points that felt genuinely macabre – not least because the events there could be authenticated – were the apartment where Sid Vicious od'd and the building that once housed The Triangle Shirtwaist Factory. It was here that the worst industrial disaster in the city's history happened, in 1911, when a fire took the lives of 146 workers, primarily because all the doors had been locked to prevent them taking unauthorised breaks or sneaking out with stolen goods.

Wanting to say our farewells to the Big Apple on a more uplifting note, we headed back to Times Square and what has become our regular nightcap venue. The rain had finally stopped and the revellers were out in full force, as we shared our impressions of the city.

When in New York…

Tricia, a first timer, is entranced by its scale, variety and energy. For myself, returning after all these years, it feels that it's been cleaned up, in every respect. I'd set off on that earlier visit with many words of warning ringing in my ears, about the physical and moral risks that New York would present, and the need to exercise great care. I won't pretend I paid much heed, apart from taking the precaution of dressing more like a mugger than a muggee, when I was out and about. But it did have the air of a city where civilisation was breaking down and Armageddon was nigh.

Every time I got on the subway, there was someone in the carriage stinking and ranting. Every street corner had at least one person offering wares that would undoubtedly have been illegal, had they been what the vendor claimed them to be. The clubs all had heavies with guns guarding the doors, and most of the clientele seemed to be driven by something more than just a love of dancing. The well-off were hiding away in offices and homes with high levels of security in place. The impoverished were unavoidable. Away from Madison, Fifth Avenue and the Upper West Side, half the buildings were either abandoned or looked like they might as well be. I survived, however, with nothing worse than fatigue and an expense account that needed some imaginative justification.

Since I'm no longer a young man, eager for adventure and willing to flirt with danger, a more sedate NYC is probably not a bad thing. I'm sure Tricia wouldn't have enjoyed the 1982 version as much as she did the 2019 revamp. For both of us, we know we've barely scratched the surface, and a return visit in the not-too-distant future will most definitely be on the agenda.

Song for the day: Bob Dylan – A Hard Rain's Gonna Fall
Dylan and Greenwich Village – check. Greenwich Village and rain – on this day, most definitely check. Hard rain and contemporary relevance – check again. In its warnings, not just about environmental damage but pollution of all kinds, not least of the social fabric and the body politic, this song resonates ever more strongly, nearly sixty years after it was written.

Day 5 - SOUTHBOUND

New York → Washington

Travel by rail, which was at the heart of the American Dream and of westward expansion for many decades, has been dying over the past century. The extent of the network, peaking at around a quarter of a million miles during the First World War, has now shrunk to less than half of that. Plans to introduce new, high speed passenger lines have consistently been postponed, abandoned or blocked, and what remains of the system is used predominantly for carrying freight.

You'd never have guessed that, though, if you'd been with us on the concourse of Penn Station at 10 o'clock on a Saturday morning. There were queues at all the ticket booths, crowds in front of the departure boards and stampedes to the gates, whenever a new opening was announced.

The last time I'd travelled from New York to Washington, I'd done it by car. Getting out of the city had taken an age, and the New Jersey Turnpike, while fabled in song, was nightmarish in real life. I couldn't have begun to emulate Paul Simon in counting the cars, which were racing bumper-to-bumper along a multiplicity of lanes, swerving between them with no apparent highway code or regard for safety. I was too focused on trying to avoid being hit.

I wasn't keen to repeat that experience, so we'd booked tickets with Amtrak, the American equivalent of British Rail. While not cheap, the prices compared favourably with the eye-watering cost of rail travel in the UK, and the journey promised to be both quicker (three hours according to the timetable) and far less stressful than the automotive alternative. Car hire and the start of the road trip proper will have to wait another couple of days.

The first half of the ride, through the built-up sprawl of New Jersey and Pennsylvania was grim - a sad illustration of rampant development that's outlived its purpose. The main impression was of waste. Huge piles of demolished or abandoned buildings and machinery left to rot. Whole neighbourhoods of housing that looked unfit for habitation, but still had signs of residents clinging on, almost certainly for lack of alternatives. And vast parking lots with absolutely nothing in them. Detroit might be the most conspicuous example of urban decay in America right now, but clearly it's not the only one.

The second half, however, was a very different story. Beyond Wilmington the track ran alongside - and sometimes across – the nooks and crannies of Chesapeake Bay for much of the way. Trees were abundant and in full leaf. Rows of wooden jetties, with little boats bobbing next to them, stretched out into the water from weekend homes, varying in size from the quaint to the grand, all with manicured lawns. The roads parallel to the railway were mostly single lane and quiet. A taste of things to come, we hope, as our journey progresses. But it felt strange, to have such beauty separated by only a few minutes and miles from what we'd seen earlier.

After the claustrophobic hubbub of New York, Washington came as a delightful contrast, from the moment we walked out of Union Station. The hordes of visitors are simply swallowed up by the acres of parkland and dwarfed by the epic scale of the surrounding buildings and monuments. Like the parts of London that rose up during the full flush of the British Empire in the 18th and 19th centuries, this is architecture and town planning that speaks of unlimited confidence and wealth.

Talking of spaciousness, our hotel also made a welcome change from the cramped quarters we'd recently vacated. In most respects it was a bog standard chain establishment, catering for folk letting down what little hair they had on corporate weekend pow-wows and bonding sessions. But our room was much more what you would expect in an American city: not one but two beds, both larger than what we'd been given in New York; a TV with a screen size that would have been more suited to a multiplex; and a bathroom that could have accommodated a post-match basketball team.

Once we'd checked in, we went over to the Capitol Building, the imposing seat of the government. On a non-working day it was deserted, apart from a couple of security guards, and we lingered for a while on the steps to admire the view down the National Mall, all the way past the Washington Monument to the Lincoln Memorial at the other end, a couple of miles distant.

The Trump government is clearly working flat out.

Apparently the Mall is the most visited of all the national parks. Considering that list includes Yosemite, Yellowstone, Niagara Falls and the Grand Canyon, this is quite some statistic. And, from where we were standing, it was hard to believe. The only part that looked remotely busy was the line of fast food vans running across the middle of the park.

We were, however, able to conjure up images of occasions when this same scene has been teeming with humanity. Some two million came to witness Barack Obama's first presidential inauguration, in January 2009, for example. (Rather less for Trump's in 2017, though naturally he denies that.) Perhaps even more memorable was the March on Washington for Jobs and Freedom, in 1963, which culminated in Martin Luther King's 'I Have A Dream' speech, delivered from in front of Lincoln's statue to an audience that filled the Mall as far as the eye could see. Events such as those would certainly give the visitor numbers a boost.

Moving on, we popped into the National Museum of the American Indian, part of the multi-faceted Smithsonian, before they closed for the day. We were happy to do this for just a few minutes because, like many of the nation's public museums, admission is free.

One section which immediately caught my attention, in the short time available to us, was labelled 'Treaties'. Given that the takeover of territory from the native peoples was characterised by greed, treachery and genocide, I was interested to see how the subject would be handled. Not too surprisingly, the curators had opted for a scholarly analysis of the interaction between two very different cultures, rather than brutal frankness or any hint of a *mea culpa*.

The catalogue of lies, broken promises and government-sanctioned displacement, which the many hundreds of treaties between the white authorities and the tribes make up, was euphemised as a failure of translation. The settlers, we were told, didn't appreciate the mindset of the Indians, and vice versa. The ambition and acquisitiveness of one side couldn't have been more at odds with philosophy of the other, for whom the land was owned by no-one and whose over-arching aim was to live in harmony with nature, rather than conquer it. As the headline for the *New York Times*' review of the exhibition put it, 'Understanding Wasn't Mutual'.

The one glimmer of light at the end of this tragic tunnel is that many of those treaties are, theoretically, still in force. There have been several instances of tribes successfully reinstating their terms, from fishing rights to sovereignty in areas officially allocated to them. We're looking forward to visiting at least a couple of those areas later in the trip.

A passage to Indians.

Going from one downtrodden ethnic minority to another, our evening took us to The Dubliner, which boasts itself to be 'America's premier Irish pub'. Given the number of citizens with Irish ancestry and the proliferation of watering holes seeking to exploit that connection, this is a bold assertation. We are, of course, in no position to confirm or dispute it. But the music and symbolism of the Emerald Isle were on full display, there were plenty of lilting Irish accents among both customers and staff, the Guinness was poured correctly and a good *craic* was had by all.

Song for the day: Green Day – American Idiot
In the town where a man uniquely unqualified for public office holds the highest position in the land (maybe even the world), and has surrounded himself with acolytes equally lacking in knowledge or any inclination to acquire it, this seems to sum up both the government and the people who voted for it pretty well.

Day 6 - BRING OUT YOUR DEAD

Washington

America has a bad habit of killing its best, one way or another. As Washington is keen to remind us. Everywhere you look, there's a monument or memorial or building, named after a late worthy or dedicated to those who died in the service of their country.

Having been ranked as the greatest POTUS ever <u>and</u> meeting his untimely end in this very town, Abe Lincoln does particularly well out of it. He's got a statue outside the Court of Appeals; the theatre where he was shot and the house where he died have become part of the National Parks Service; and his memorial, a neo-classical hulk at the southern end of the Mall, makes him the monolithic master of all he surveys.

We did the tour of the Ford Theatre and the Petersen House, a former boarding house on the opposite side of the street… yet another free attraction, although we had to book a time slot, to be sure of getting in. The tour was billed as including a presentation by a park ranger. We expected this to be a straight recitation of facts from a government functionary. What we got was an extraordinary monologue, compellingly performed on the stage of the theatre, in the persona of the man who claimed to have killed Lincoln's assassin, John Wilkes Booth - the Jack Ruby of the piece, if you like.

This man, Boston Corbett (no, we'd never heard of him either), was in the regiment dispatched to follow Wilkes Booth when he fled from Washington. They eventually cornered him, in a barn on a tobacco farm in Virginia. When it looked as if he was going to fire on his pursuers, he was fatally shot – supposedly by Corbett – despite orders to take him alive. Like the president, he took several hours to die.

The scene of another crime.

Corbett was an eccentric character, to put it kindly. Mad as a fish might be a more accurate description. A religious fanatic, he had castrated himself with a pair of scissors to avoid temptations of the flesh; his army career was punctuated by disruptive behavior and disciplinary action; and he later spent time in an insane asylum. There were always questions as to whether he really was the man who shot Wilkes Booth, but he achieved some notoriety after the event and even turned that into income by giving lectures on the subject. ("Nobody asked him back a second time", it's reported, "His wild incoherencies were too much.") He may not have been the obvious choice, as the focal point for telling the story of the assassination, but he was certainly a memorable one.

We stayed on, after the theatre had cleared, and spoke with the ranger. It turned out that he and his colleagues, who deliver the presentations, are allowed to do it any way they please. It would have been interesting to see how they compared. But that would have involved a lot more standing in line and, as we've already established, queuing is not our favourite pastime.

One good thing that came out of the queuing we did do, however, was a reminder of just how friendly and open Americans are, once you're outside New York. While waiting to get into the theatre and while sitting in it, before the ranger's presentation, we were engaged in conversations with our neighbours, which would almost certainly have led to a full exchange of life stories, had time allowed. We'll look forward to further such encounters.

From a dead president to a brain-dead president. Our next port of call was The White House. As a citizen of the country that voted for Brexit, I'm not in the best position to criticise the American people's decision to elect a philandering, sociopathic, narcissistic con artist as their main man. Some will suggest that, as I'm not American, it's none of my goddamn business. My counter would be that since "when America sneezes, the rest of the world catches cold" and with POTUS also being the self-appointed leader of the free world, the conduct and character of whoever holds that position is justifiably everyone's concern.

Which brings us to another relevant issue that's often raised – usually by people who can afford to seek injunctions, preventing the media from giving their dirty linen a good airing. They argue that their private lives are of no relevance to what they do in the wider world, and therefore should be of no public interest. As if being consistently dishonest or dishonourable towards your supposed loved ones or close associates isn't going to be a good indication of how you'll behave in other respects. Especially if, as in the case of Messrs. Trump and Johnson, there's no hint of shame or embarrassment when your misdeeds are revealed. (Btw – isn't it a delicious irony that one is named after a fart and the other a prick?)

Walking over to the Lincoln Memorial, we passed a small, grey stone cottage that was quite out of keeping with all the huge public buildings that line the rest of the Mall. This is the Lockkeeper's House, which previously stood on the short lived and long disappeared Washington Canal. A plaque announced that it had recently been relocated and renovated, at a cost of several million dollars. We assumed it had been moved from another part of the city, to a place where it could be more readily appreciated. So we were astonished to find out that it had actually been shifted barely twelve yards. Why this was worth all the trouble and expense remains a mystery.

A great man. And a statue of Abe Lincoln.

The Lincoln Memorial finally made sense of those National Parks visitor numbers. The steps up to it and the 'temple' that houses the statue were rammed. Avoiding having your eye poked out by a carelessly wielded selfie stick became a priority.

Usually, when taking souvenir photos, Tricia is insistent on having no interlopers in shot, giving the impression that we have the attraction or landmark or beauty spot to ourselves. You would have thought that, in this instance, this would be mission impossible, as she tried to capture me and Abe undisturbed. But that would be to underestimate her determination as a photographer and (more surprisingly) my patience as a model. With the moment finally captured to her satisfaction, we inched our way out through the throng, happy in the knowledge that the next week or so of our journey would be infinitely more tranquil.

A taste of that tranquility was almost immediately found at the World War II Memorial, midway between the Lincoln Memorial and the Washington Monument. It's an expansive combination of pillars, arches and fountains, with a wall containing 4000 gold stars, commemorating the 400,000 American lives lost during the conflict. Despite being much more affecting than the Lincoln equivalent, it was obviously considered less photogenic, as we did have it almost to ourselves.

We were starving by now and turned our steps towards Old Ebbitt Grill, a long established and highly rated Washington restaurant, which has counted several occupants of the nearby White House among its customers, over the years. Unfortunately its fame meant that folk were queuing down the street to get in. A sixty minutes wait for tables, even at a quite early hour, was announced and our stomachs told us to move on.

A little further along, we came across Harry's Pub. Which was nowhere near as grand or illustrious as Ebbitt's, but was actually far more our kind of place. Through the windows we could see old style bar stools, baseball on the TV, homely waitresses and a clientele who looked like they came from the neighbourhood, rather than from a tour bus. That, along with a menu offering all the choices you'd expect from such an establishment, at reasonable prices, was more than enough to draw us in.

After a couple of hours spent consuming first rate burgers and soda with free refills (one of this country's better innovations), and eavesdropping on the locals at the bar venting opinions on everything from pitching techniques to politics, we felt we'd covered much of the span of American history and society in the space of a single day.

Song for the day: Marvin Gaye – 'Abraham, Martin and John'
Marvin didn't write this song, nor was he the first to record it, but this is the sublime version that most people recognise. What would we give to have leaders of this calibre again? And can you imagine anyone adding a verse praising the Donald in like terms? Even his most rabid supporters would probably think that a step too far.

Day 7 - INTO THE WILD

Washington → Skyline Drive

Today was the day when this trip started in earnest. Big cities and public transport are all very well – in small doses – but the two of us, a car and the open road are what it's really about. In a perfect cinematic world, that car would be a vintage Caddy convertible. But since reliability and cost have to be factored in, our companion for the next five weeks will be an unromantic but hopefully fit-for-purpose Japanese saloon.

We got off to a mixed start. We were given an attractively priced upgrade by the very friendly guy at the car hire desk, who was horrified at the prospect of us intending to drive several thousand miles, across mountains and deserts, in a compact vehicle. To be honest, we'd anticipated this and correctly believed that, during an off-peak period, we'd be offered a better deal at the collection point than we'd get from the online price list.

As we reached the exit, however, in a particularly cramped corner of the underground garage, the lady checking us out noticed that the license on our chosen vehicle would expire during our unusually long rental period. We'd have to be given another one. Which was less straightforward than you might have expected, as a queue had already formed behind us on the narrow approach to the exit and we were unable to move.

Several minutes of confusion ensued, with a cacophonous accompaniment of honking horns and the angry voices of other drivers, as they were moved back to allow our replacement to be brought through. We then had to transfer everything over, before we could be on our way. (A few days later, we realised that the paperwork for the rental was still in the first car, which would make things more complicated when we came to the end of the hire.)

For the first couple of hours our US-friendly satnav (courtesy of No.4 son, George, who travelled around the States as a football coach for several months in 2013) was a boon, as it guided us through the maze of freeways, highways, toll roads and state roads out of Washington. Eventually, however, we were able to cast it aside. For the next six hundred miles we'll be making our way south down Skyline Drive and the Blue Ridge Parkway, effectively one continuous, single carriageway road, running along the spine of the Appalachian Mountains. Both were created in the '30s, as projects to provide work during the Great Depression. Both feature prominently among 'The Most Scenic Drives In America'.

The term 'parkway' was originally intended to refer to landscaped roads through scenic areas, sympathetically constructed for leisure purposes. Commercial traffic wouldn't be allowed on them and speeds would be restricted, allowing for maximum enjoyment both of the driving and of the surroundings. That's no longer the case. America is now full of roads called 'parkways' which are indistinguishable from any other hideous, soulless, life-threatening freeway. Parkway East in Pittsburgh, for example, is better known for its traffic jams and wretched state of repair, than for any aesthetic virtues. And I don't remember the Arroyo Seco Parkway, which links Pasadena and LA, with any fondness at all. The ones we're about to follow are part of the earlier dream, however, and if the first afternoon is anything to go by, we're in for a treat. Panoramic viewpoints and enticing trails are so numerous that you have to pick and choose which ones to pause at or follow, otherwise you'd spend all day getting nowhere.

Having read Bill Bryson's 'A Walk In The Woods', a chronicle of his attempts to negotiate stretches of the Appalachian Trail, a pathway which follows much the same route through the mountains as the roads we'll be taking, we were particularly excited by the prospect of seeing bears in their natural habitat. Bryson, true to form, plays them for comic effect, feigning terror at the prospect of meeting one while camped in the back of beyond and recounting horror stories as if they were daily occurrences. Since no-one else was passing through the ranger post, when we arrived at the start of Skyline Drive, we sought information from what seemed likely to be a more reliable source: the ranger on duty.

He was non-committal about the likelihood of coming across a bear. "If'n Lady Luck's smilin' on yer", was the best he could manage. But he was more forthcoming on what to do if an encounter became too close. Running away would be futile. Bears can outpace Usain Bolt without breaking sweat, and they climb trees far better than we do. The suggestion, if you're not carrying a gun, is to make a lot of noise and wave your arms about, making yourself seem as large and intimidating as possible. Which might conceivably work for me, being six feet tall and on the hefty side, but may be less successful for someone of Tricia's petite size. The bear is supposed to retreat at this point, but if it doesn't follow the script and you find yourself in hand-to-claw combat, the only advice was to "fight back". We both fervently hoped that we'd never need to follow this course of action.

If you go down to the woods today...

We'd barely gone five minutes down the road, when we saw a couple of vehicles parked on the verge and the occupants pointing their lenses into the woods. On joining them, we realised that Lady Luck had wasted no time in deciding to smile on us. A bear was ambling about, only fifty yards away, snuffling among the bushes and around the trunks of trees. Their diet consists mostly of grasses, roots, berries and insects rather than tourists, according to information boards along the route. Which presumably is what it was intent on finding, as it paid us no attention and seemed undisturbed by the machine gun clatter of multiple camera shutters. When it finally moved deeper into the woods, out of sight, we resumed our journey, congratulating ourselves on our good fortune.

Our bed for the night was at Skyland, a rustic 'resort' established in the 1890s, well before Skyline Drive was conceived, and only developed as a resort because the copper mining company, which previously owned the land, wasn't making a profit and the owners were desperate to find another use for it. It's expanded since then. It now has over 170 rooms in wooden cabins scattered among the trees, plus a pleasant dining room and bar. Despite being a Monday night in late April and the road being exceptionally quiet, it was fully booked. Thankfully one of the reservations was ours. We lucked out again and got a room with a fabulous outlook.

Our bed for the night was at Skyland, a rustic 'resort' established in the 1890s, well before Skyline Drive was conceived, and only developed as a resort because the copper mining company, which previously owned the land, wasn't making a profit and the owners were desperate to find another use for it. It's expanded since then. It now has over 170 rooms in wooden cabins scattered among the trees, plus a pleasant dining room and bar. Despite being a Monday night in late April and the road being exceptionally quiet, it was fully booked. Thankfully one of the reservations was ours. We lucked out again and got a room with a fabulous outlook.

There was enough daylight left for a short hike to the top of the nearby Stony Man Mountain (at over 4000 ft, the second highest peak in Shenandoah National Park, but the car had already done most of the climb). A sign at the start of the trail warned of the presence of timber rattlesnakes, which immediately rang alarm bells for Tricia. They're venomous, although deaths from bites are very rare. More positively, they have a long period of hibernation (or brumation, to use the correct term) during the colder months, which were only just coming to an end at this altitude. On balance, it seemed safe to proceed with due caution. Which, so far as Tricia was concerned, meant scuttling away from any sound or movement, real or imagined, coming from the undergrowth.

Into the great wide open.

On returning to our room, I sat on the balcony while Tricia had a catnap, to watch the sun go down over the other side of the Shenandoah Valley below. With cigar and wine in hand, and only the birds, the breeze and distant train whistles as a soundtrack, it was one of those moments when life feels blessed.

We decided to spend the evening in the bar of Skyland, rather than the restaurant, and were glad we did. We hadn't set our expectations high. Being the only game in town all too often results in prices that are out of kilter with standards, and reviews of the place had been mixed. But we needn't have worried. Everything from the down-home service to the BBQ chicken wings was tip top. They even had Samuel Adams Boston Lager, my preferred American beer thus far.

A small arsenal of acoustic stringed instruments was perched in one corner of the room when we arrived, indicating that live music was also on the menu. This isn't always a good thing, but in this instance it was a delight. We'd barely sat down when a forty something couple stepped up and proceeded to entertain us, for the next couple of hours, with a mixture of country, folk and bluegrass songs and instrumentals, stories about the music and themselves, and banter with the fully engaged audience. It was right up my street, and in this setting it was perfect. New York and Washington already felt a million miles away.

Song for the day: The Carter Family – 'Mid The Green Fields Of Virginia'
The Carter Family had to go to Tennessee and Texas to find fame, but they hailed from Virginia and were instrumental (literally) in taking the songs and sounds of these mountains to the nation. They created a deep well – and a multi-generational legacy – from which much of the music I love most has been drawn.

Day 8 - FOOD, GLORIOUS FOOD

Skyline Drive

On a day of clean mountain air and countless magnificent views, the two main points of note came at the start and end of it, and both involved food for the body rather than the soul.

A big decision awaited us when we woke up. Should we have breakfast at Skyland, before ascending Hawksbill, at 4051ft the highest point in the Shenandoah National Park? Or should we wait till later, and get something at Big Meadows, the next point of civilisation along Skyline Drive? Despite the tempting prospect of an al fresco table on the terrace at Big Meadows, we opted to take sustenance in anticipation of the endeavour ahead, and we were bloody glad we did.

Not because the hike was the most demanding thing we've ever done, but because the Lodge at Big Meadows hasn't yet opened for the season. The best we could do, to reward ourselves for our efforts, was a cup of coffee and a Sprite from a dispensing machine at the ranger station. Which compared very unfavourably with the ample breakfast we'd enjoyed earlier.

Hawksbill Mountain ranks high among Trip Advisor's list of Things To Do in the Shenandoah National Park. Reviewers have called it "a great hike", "richly rewarding" and "breathtaking". At first, we couldn't see why. The path from the car park meandered ever upwards, through phalanxes of trees that blocked out any possibility of views. We could have been in the woods of the Chiltern Hills, much closer to home, were it not for the steep angle of ascent. Our thigh muscles, still in the habit of walking on flat city streets, started to complain.

Then we reached the top and everything became clear – quite literally, as we'd been gifted a day with good visibility, even if the wind was uncomfortably brisk, once away from the shelter of the trees. The series of rocky outcrops, which comprise the summit, offered panoramas that stretched to infinity in every direction: along the thickly wooded Blue

Ridge range; across to the Allegheny Mountains, on the western side of the Shenandoah Valley; and down to fertile farmland below. We were only too happy to drink them in, while we gave our legs a chance to recover.

On top of old Hawksbill.

Skyline Drive is barely 100 miles long, but it has an outstanding viewpoint (or 'overlook', as they're known in these parts) for almost every one of those miles. That, and the 35mph speed limit, mean it can't be rushed. It was late afternoon before we saw the sign telling us that we'd reached its southern end.

For a few jarring moments we were back in the maelstrom of the 21st century, on the stretch of I-64 that runs through the short gap in the mountains, between the end of Skyline Drive and the start of the Blue Ridge Parkway. The multiple lanes were filled with vehicles, including lots of monster trucks, all travelling at what felt like insane speed after our leisurely progress along the ridgeway, and the road was flanked with a cluster of chain eateries and motels, none of them enticing.

We later found out that this section of freeway is a notorious accident blackspot, with several instances of appalling multi-vehicle pile-ups over the years, because of its proneness to sudden thick fog. There was no sign of that during our very brief visit, but we were still relieved to be turning off after a couple of miles.

The end of the first Scenic Drive.

Our destination for the night was a B&B in the town of Afton in Rockfish Valley, on the eastern side of the mountains. The map on their website showed them as being right on the main drag (Route 6), which runs through the middle of town. As it turned out, Route 6 is a winding country lane and Afton is nothing more than a few modest dwellings, scattered over quite a wide area. It does, however, number the singer/songwriter Mary Chapin Carpenter among its handful of residents. Which is a huge claim to fame, in my book. Please check her out, if you're not already familiar.

We drove through Afton several times before we spotted an identifying name board by the entrance to the B&B. At the end of a mile-long dirt track, we arrived at a random collection of uninspiring buildings with the obligatory ancient pick-up parked outside. I was half expecting a man with a long beard, no teeth and a weapon to appear, as I got out of the car to investigate.

In fact there was no sign of life, but the door of the main building was open, so I ventured inside. The transformation was reminiscent of riads we've stayed at in Morocco, where what looks to be ramshackle from the outside is revealed as having an interior of some splendour. A room key was hanging on the wall with our name above it, so we assumed we'd come to the right place. The owners, apparently, were out for the day.

Tricia was still concerned that we were miles from any obvious source of food and would almost certainly go to bed hungry, unless we wanted to brave a return to the I-64. But a further big plus for our temporary home was unexpectedly fast wifi. We put it to full use in researching the subject of places to eat, while we chilled out in the spacious lounge area and sampled the homemade cookies, which had thoughtfully been provided alongside the coffee-making facilities.

Not knowing when we would next have such good connectivity, we also took the opportunity to check in with the family back home. It struck me how different things were, when I went on a summer-long hitchhiking jaunt round Europe, between school and university in the early '70s. Back then, my parents were lucky to get a postcard every few weeks, letting them know where I was and reassuring them that I was still alive, eating properly and not in jail or being held hostage by one of the terror groups, who were active in Europe at the time.

These days, with almost every point on the globe a mere click away from any other point and high res video links treated as a given, rather than a technological miracle, there's no such escape for young travellers. They can cross the world, in search of independence and adventure, but mum and dad will probably be alerting the authorities if they go incommunicado for more than a couple of days. Whether or not this is a good thing, I'll leave you to decide.

Of the limited dining options we were able to identify, in this very rural setting, one stood out. The Blue Mountain Brewery was a five minutes' drive away and, when we arrived, the pub attached to it was clearly a popular place. The garden was full of folk tucking into plates of what looked like good food and chattering away. We joined them and spent a very pleasant evening, giving the brewery's products a thorough taste test, watching the locals at play and gazing out on the mountains we'd just passed through. Oh, and the fries that accompanied our BBQ pulled pork sandwiches were probably the best we've ever had, anywhere. A happy ending, indeed.

Song for the day: Mary Chapin Carpenter – 'Goodnight America'
Since we're resting our heads in her hometown, this seems very apt. Mary has written a number of songs that capture the spirit of travelling the open roads of this vast land, in search of something that always seems just out of reach. This is one of the best.

Day 9 - IN THE BLUE RIDGE MOUNTAINS OF VIRGINIA

Blue Ridge Parkway

We woke to a world of mist. The mountains, so glorious as the sun was setting on the previous evening, had completely disappeared. Even at 10 o'clock, after we'd had an unhurried breakfast, the fog we'd been warned about was engulfing I-64 and visibility was barely twenty yards in places. We proceeded with extreme caution and prayed that others would be doing the same. It was no better when we turned onto the Blue Ridge Parkway, but we seemed to be the only vehicle on it and we consoled ourselves with the thought that any collisions here would happen at a very low speed.

A day of ponderous and unrewarding driving beckoned, as we inched our way uphill. Then suddenly, like a plane rising above the clouds to infinite blue skies, we emerged into sunlight and things just got better from there on.

Although the Parkway is a continuation of Skyline Drive, some differences soon became apparent. On the Drive the trees above 3000ft were still bare whereas here, even at 4000 ft, they're in full leaf. Who knew there were so many shades of green? Or that the climate would change so quickly as we move south?

Another difference is that the Parkway has such an abundance of natural and man-made attractions that places, which would usually be rated as 'must see' and have at least a cafe and gift shop attached, barely get a mention in guide books and sometimes aren't even signed when you're there.

The Farm Museum at Humpback Rocks is an insight into what it had been like, for folk trying to eke out a subsistence living in these unpromising surroundings - a way of life that continued deep into the 20th century, before the mountains became a playground for visitors. A collection of structures from the 19th century, a log cabin and a variety of outbuildings, have been taken from the surrounding area and reassembled here. One of them was a bear-proof pigpen, where a sign warned us not to venture too close, as a rattlesnake had taken up residence. We're not in The Chilterns now, as a second sighting of a bear, later in the day, would remind us!

As we were the only people there, it was quite easy to sit on the porch of the cabin and imagine the isolation of mountain farmsteads such as this. And the rigours of a day-to-day existence where even the most basic needs, from getting water to starting a fire, involved a chore. The best you can say for it, is that it must have been a reasonably healthy lifestyle. William J. Carter, after whom the farm is named, survived well into his eighties, as did his father. But it must also have been cramped, if the single room cabin we were seeing was typical. William was one of eight children that his parents produced.

My log cabin home in the sky

A couple of hours later, Wigwam Falls was another lovely surprise. Just a stone's throw from the road, yet with no announcement and therefore no-one around, it's actually more a series of cascades than a waterfall. But with winter and the snow melt not long past, it was still a lively spectacle. The water tumbled down under a disused narrow-gauge railway track, part of a 50-mile line serving the logging industry, which had been very active in the early years of the 20th century. We lingered a while to enjoy the peaceful surroundings, take pictures and drink from the stream – the water was chilled to perfection and delicious.

In fact the Parkway as a whole is unbelievably quiet. Several miles can go by, without seeing another vehicle. In this respect it was reminiscent of our trek across the Australian outback, but without the dead kangaroos.

A little further on the road dropped down to the valley of the James River. This was both broad and beautiful, with thickly wooded banks reflecting in the water. As someone who does voluntary education and preservation work on the Grand Union Canal back home, however, I was more interested in the James River & Kanawha Canal. A footbridge, running directly beneath the bridge carrying the Parkway, took us from the visitors' centre to the other side of the river, where a remaining section of canal would be found, along with a restored lock.

If you've bought into the notion that anything draped in the stars'n'stripes is, by definition, bigger and better than what anywhere else has to show, the James River & Kanawha Canal – and particularly this lock, which had been deemed worthy of restoration - will give that the lie.

Call that a lock?

The locks that I'm familiar with are substantial constructions, precision built to take two 70ft narrowboats side by side. The lock gates, made of heavy timbers and thick metal, are expected to withstand decades of pressure, often inclement weather and persistent use. What I was looking at now would only accommodate one small vessel, while the gates were consistent with everything else that I could see of the canal – flimsy little brothers, when compared to their sturdy Brit equivalents. I wasn't surprised to learn that plans for the waterway never got completed and it had fallen out of use soon after the Civil War.

86 miles south, from the start of the Parkway, the Peaks of Otter are a group of three mountains – Sharp Top, Flat Top and Harkening Hill – surrounding a lake that was created in the '60s, to replace a large boggy meadow. On one shore of the lake is the Peaks of Otter Lodge, our home for the night, created at around the same time - a run of bedroom blocks and a main building, containing the reception area, a gift shop, a restaurant and a bar. At first glance it could have been an expensive private care home. Most of the guests, sitting on their balconies or on benches by the water, looked like they were waiting for staff to take them to the dining room or help them into bed. But we had an uninterrupted view over the lake and mountains, and the biggest room of the trip thus far, so we weren't complaining.

With sunshine and mountains beckoning, we had to choose which of the three Peaks we would tackle for our evening constitutional. If we'd had a full day at our disposal, we would almost certainly have gone for Sharp Top, the tallest of them and celebrated for its 360° outlooks. But, as the name suggests, it's also by far the steepest, so the most demanding and time-consuming climb. Not wanting to risk ending the day knackered or, worse, being stuck out in the woods when darkness fell, we opted for Harkening Hill. At nearly five miles long this trail would still be a proper hike, but one that we should certainly be able to complete in the couple of hours available before twilight.

To be honest, the views that greeted us, when we reached the summit, were far from the best we've enjoyed in these mountains. Surrounding trees got in the way and thousands more were pretty much all we could see between them. What we came across on the way up was more memorable.

The Balance Rock is one of those geological freaks, which has somehow left a large piece of stone (about the size of a transit van, in this instance) poised on top of a much smaller one. It looks precarious, but has probably been there for hundreds, if not thousands of years. Wikipedia lists a whole host of such formations in various parts of the world, but this one isn't among them, despite being at least as impressive as some of those that are. In fact it gets little attention even here. It's situated off the main trail, with minimal signage, and it's not too easy to find. Photos making it seem as if we were holding it in place with our fingertips were, of course, obligatory.

We had the woods to ourselves, apart from the birds, so we were startled when the silence was suddenly broken by the sounds of snapping twigs, disturbed foliage and heavy breathing. A large black bear came galloping down the hill from our left, crossed the path barely thirty yards ahead of us, and disappeared among the trees below. After pausing to make sure he/she wasn't coming back, we proceeded on heightened alert, wondering if our walking poles would be up to the job of defending us against an attack.

The last bit of the trail back to base was called Elk Run, which led us to believe we might add to our wildlife spotting for the day. We didn't and when we enquired at reception, we were told that elk, which once roamed the land in huge herds, had been hunted almost to extinction in the Appalachians by the end of the 18th century. There was more positive news, however. They'd been successfully re-introduced to the Great Smoky Mountains, in Tennessee, a few hundred miles further south, and were now being found once again in the lower reaches of the Blue Ridge Mountains. So we'll live in hope.

By the time we'd finished the hike, freshened up and wandered over to the restaurant at the Lodge, it was deserted, apart from staff tidying up and preparing for breakfast service. Even though it was only 8 o'clock, the other residents had obviously already been fed, medicated and tucked up in bed. Our waitress was amiable and attentive, but we couldn't help detecting a sense of disappointment that the end of her evening's work was being delayed.

Song for the day: John Otway & Wild Willy Barrett – 'Misty Mountain'

This is a shameless excuse to name check a couple of characters who I attempted to manage for a while, back in my misspent youth. The song wasn't written about the Blue Ridge Mountains. In fact it was inspired by the Chiltern Hills, a modest range in the south east of England. While the Chilterns are very lovely, they're no-one's idea of mountainous. But we've spent some of the day "way up on a misty high mountain, far away from the dusty, dirty town", so I feel entitled to use it. And Willy's old time fiddle playing is in a direct line of descent from these parts.

Day 10 - COME RAIN, COME SHINE

Blue Ridge Parkway

Unlike Skyline Drive, which is part of the Shenandoah National Park, where Mother Nature is largely untouched, the Blue Ridge Parkway co-exists with the world of Man. Large areas of forest have been cleared for pasture (although nothing like as much as in the early 1900s, when over-zealous loggers apparently took out more trees than they left). Even at higher levels we've been passing by prosperous looking farms, as well as long abandoned shacks and barns. The Parkway also intersects at regular intervals with state roads, so dawdling sightseers have to share it with locals keen to get about their business. It was still pretty quiet though – maybe another car every half mile, on average.

The day started well, with breakfast overlooking the lake and mountains at the Peaks of Otter Lodge, and then a visit to Mabry Mill – an historic site so photogenic that other states have appropriated it in their own tourism-boosting efforts! Even more popular was the Mabry Mill Restaurant, on the opposite side of the creek that provided water for the mill, where Ed Mabry sawed timber and ground grain in the first half of the 20th century. This was absolutely packed, as was the car park outside. It seemed bizarre that, having encountered virtually no traffic on the way there, the world and his wife should have appeared out of nowhere, as soon as the opportunity to eat presented itself.

While they engaged in America's favourite pastime of piling on the pounds (anyone who thinks it's baseball is kidding themselves) we were able to look round the various buildings on display and take our pics undisturbed. With warm sunshine and the surrounding trees coming into full leaf, and no risk of being photobombed, we felt we were seeing the place at its very best.

Mabry Mill in Virginia (whatever anyone else may try to tell you!).

Things soon changed though, as they're wont to do at higher reaches. The next couple of hours were spent driving through rain, which was of monsoon proportions at times, and visibility which varied from poor to unnerving.

This unhappy stretch of the journey was made even worse by the first and hopefully the last significant disappointment of the trip. The Blue Ridge Music Center was supposed to be one of our main ports of call in these parts. We were looking forward (or at least, I was) to exploring the exhibits at The American Roots Museum and hearing some of the ancient music, that seeped out of these hills to enter ears nationwide and change the world. We never imagined that, in the first week of May, the Center would be shut. For reasons best known to themselves, they don't open for the season until next weekend.

When we stopped to console ourselves with coffee, at a country store a little further down the road, the lady who served us complained bitterly about the inability of the various attractions and other establishments along the Parkway to co-ordinate their opening dates. She reckons it causes much frustration – even distress, if the lodge or camping ground you were expecting to use is still closed. We wholeheartedly agreed.

The same lady was interested in our travel plans and seemed astonished to hear how many states we expected to be passing through. We counted them off, from east to west, and it came to nearly twenty. She, in middle age, was embarrassed to admit she had been to only four, including her native Virginia. Which isn't at all unusual. The average American visits twelve in his or her lifetime and fewer than 50% have passports, so never venture outside the country. Small wonder that Trumplethinskin's isolationist policies meet with widespread approval. You only have to watch the news, on any channel here, to realise that there's minimal interest in the rest of the world and minimal coverage of it, unless America or Americans are directly involved.

Our next stop was another one of those places that go unnoticed by the vast majority of travellers. As we pulled in by the Puckett Cabin, I told Tricia there was a sad story attached to it. Knowing nothing whatsoever about it, she said she had a sense of a child of our granddaughter Freja's age (she would shortly be celebrating her third birthday). There were no obvious clues to inspire this feeling – we were looking at a small, two storey wooden house, fronted by an area of grass enclosed by old wooden fencing. The information board was too far away to be read, at this point.

In fact, the cabin commemorates 'Aunt' Orelena Hawke Puckett, born in 1837. A lady who lost twenty four (24!) of her own children before they turned three. She went on to become the neighbourhood midwife, delivering the last of over a thousand babies shortly before she died at the age of 102. Somewhat creeped out by Tricia's premonition, we continued on our way.

A mother pays her respects to an Aunt.

As we'd only spent thirty seconds at the Blue Ridge Music Center, as opposed to the expected two or three hours, we arrived at our final destination for the day ahead of time. But that was OK. The weather had changed again when we reached our hotel, in the heart of Blowing Rock's 'Historic Downtown', so we were happy to explore.

You have to remember, of course, that 'historic' in the United States can mean pretty much anything prior to the start of the '60s. Our house, built in 1881, would probably be classified as a national monument or museum – a centrepiece of Historic Downtown Rickmansworth. But Blowing Rock was still very pleasant.

For a town with a permanent population of just over a thousand, it seemed quite large. Until we realised that the majority of the many buildings were hotels, B&Bs, restaurants, cafes, bars, boutiques, gift shops or outdoor activity suppliers. As one of the few communities of any size actually on the Parkway, Blowing Rock has done a good job of marketing itself as 'The Crown Of The Blue Ridge' and seems to be a magnet for tourism of all kinds, from spa weekends to extreme sports.

Of all these outlets, the one I was most delighted to come across was a pub where I could have a cigar with a beer, without being in violation of local laws and risking a fine.

Smoking rules in the USA vary enormously, not just from state to state but even from town to town. In the South, where the freedom to do anything you damned well please is generally seen as a part of man's birth right, they tend to be more relaxed. Oklahoma and Virginia have zero legislated smoking bans, at the last reckoning. In California, on the other hand, you can buy tobacco but good luck with finding anywhere to use it. Smoking in, or even near, a building (including your own home, if it's rented) or a public space will probably be prohibited. Lighting up in the great outdoors is even more of a no-no, due to the real risk of starting a fire that consumes a whole county.

North Carolina, where we are now, falls somewhere in between these extremes. Their laws aren't the most draconian, but they do forbid smoking in most bars and restaurants. To my great joy, the Blowing Rock Ale House, just along the street from our hotel, had a fine selection of beers and a terrace with tables which, the barmaid assured me, was exempt from the ban because it wasn't actually in the bar. "Fill yer boots, son", slurred the gentleman slumped next to me, while I was placing our order. I was about to quip that I prefer drinking from a bottle or a glass, when I realised he had already returned to insensibility.

We went to another pub – The Six Pence – for dinner. This also had an outside area, but darkness had fallen, along with the temperature, by the time we got there. Even the possibility of a post-prandial smoke failed to make eating under the stars seem attractive, so we went inside. The place claims to be "an authentic English pub". This was backed up by Union Jacks and various items of Brit iconography and memorabilia, on display around the walls, and a large collection of ceramic beer jugs behind the bar, depicting the heads of historic English figures from Henry VIII to Churchill. Real ale, a dart board and a cloth-capped local propping up the bar with his dog at his feet, which I would have considered more convincing marks of authenticity, were not in evidence.

The menu also read like a fairly typical American affair – 'sandwiches' meant burgers, things were broiled rather than grilled and, although it offered bangers & mash, it also featured 'Welch Rarebit'. The food we had was good, though, and the service – at the table, something else you wouldn't usually find in an authentic English pub – smacked more of America in a positive way, being eager to please rather than giving the impression you were being granted a favour.

Song for the day: The Dillards – 'Old Man At The Mill'

The Dillards, formed by brothers Doug and Rodney, actually came from Missouri, but much of their music – instrumentally and vocally – has its roots in these mountains. Doug left the band before this song was recorded and went on to have an illustrious career in his own right, working with the afore-mentioned Gene Clark, among others. We'd hoped to interview him for our film about Gene, but sadly he was too ill to do it and died not long afterwards. Rodney is still playing, though, aged 81 at the time of writing.

Day 11 - THREE FALLS, NO SUBMISSIONS

Blue Ridge Parkway

We woke up in Blowing Rock and will be sleeping in Spruce Pine. The early American settlers certainly had a good way with names, as our journey will no doubt continue to demonstrate.

There were barely fifty miles of driving between the two places, which left us plenty of time to explore a couple of notable landmarks along the Parkway: the Moses H. Cone Memorial Park, just outside Blowing Rock; and Linville Falls, a series of three torrents on the river of the same name, which become increasingly impressive as the water makes its way down through a gorge.

Mr Cone was a man well worthy of being commemorated. From quite humble beginnings, as the son of German immigrants who ran a grocery store in Tennessee, he made a huge fortune manufacturing and innovating in the textile business. In the early 1900s the Cone Mills Corporation, mostly based in North Carolina, was the biggest supplier of denim in the world.

Much of that fortune ended up being devoted to conservation and philanthropy, but a fair chunk of it was spent on buying and developing the land that's now the Memorial Park and on building Flat Top Manor. This is a 20-room, colonial revival style house in a magnificent setting, 4500 feet up, looking out over landscaped gardens, meadows, orchards and lakes. All the materials for the construction, and all the furnishings, had to be brought up the mountain on carts pulled by oxen.

Sadly, Moses and his wife had no children to fill the family home, and he passed away not long after it was completed, at the age of 51. And in the short time left to him, the manor could only be used during the summer months, as it was mostly snowbound in winter. His widow did reap the fruits of his labour, however, living at Flat Top for another 39 years until she died in 1947, when it was turned into a hospital. It's now run by the National Park Service and includes a craft gallery that exhibits the work of artists from the area. Sitting on the porch, surveying all he had mastered, we could only hope that Moses had found time to enjoy some taste of the pleasure we were experiencing.

Linville River and the Falls are named after Captain William Linville, a friend of the legendary frontiersman Daniel Boone. Linville came to this region with his son John on a hunting trip in 1766. They were attacked while sleeping by Indians, who shot them, killed them and scalped them (ideally, for their sake, in that order). A third person – a boy of sixteen, who had been taken along to cook and keep camp for them – was wounded but managed to escape. The incident sounds like terrible bad luck, at first hearing, but apparently the whole area was a hotbed of conflict at the time, between rival bands of Indians, between Indians and whites, and between British troops and would-be settlers. So maybe the Linvilles were inviting trouble by going on a jolly.

'The Grand Canyon of the Southern Appalachians', apparently!

Judging from the size of the parking lot at the visitor centre, the Falls are a popular spot - as they should be - but it was almost empty for the duration of our stay. We followed the trails along the rim of the gorge, stopping at the various vantage points, and finally reached Erwin's View, overlooking the last and largest of the falls.

The hike is described as 'strenuous' by the National Park Service website. It wasn't. Not remotely. We could only imagine that the NPS are protecting themselves against possible complaints from the kind of people who get out of breath, just carrying a laden tray to their table from an 'all you can eat' buffet. Americans are extraordinarily litigious and will claim injury to their mental or physical health at the least provocation. There are several lists online of the most ridiculous lawsuits, and most of them emanate from the USA. My personal favourite is Pearson v Chung, in which a man (a judge, would you believe?) in Washington DC took action for 'inconvenience and mental anguish' against a laundry, who had mislaid a pair of his trousers. The garment was soon found and returned to its owner, but that didn't stop Mr Pearson spending four years going through the courts, in pursuit of $67 million in damages (yes, you read that right… $67,000,000). He lost the case, you might be pleased to hear, and wasn't re-appointed as a judge when his term of office expired.

We've tried in vain to find out how Erwin's View got its name. There is a town called Erwin in North Carolina, but it's over 200 miles away, on the other side of the state. You certainly wouldn't get a view of it from the Falls. A more likely suspect might be a certain Colonel Alexander Erwin, born 1749 and died 1829. He was a notable public figure in Burke County, in which Linville Falls is situated, and he's buried less than 30 miles distant.

A young man, perched on a rock at the top of the trail, was unable to shed any definitive light on the matter. But he did tell us that he lived locally and came up to this spot several times a week to sit in quiet contemplation, as he believed it was good for the soul. We weren't about to dispute the idea. Common sense, if not personal experience, would suggest that being in the great outdoors is indeed beneficial. Especially if you're in a particularly lovely or spectacular bit of the outdoors, as the three of us were.

You don't need to trust your instincts on this point, however. Science has proved it. A whole range of studies have demonstrated that interaction with nature does everything from reducing blood pressure and anxiety to improving respiratory and cardiovascular conditions, and even shows a clear effect on mental disorders such as ADHD. In fact, it's been given a name: ecotherapy. We'll be spending quite a lot of our time on this trip self-medicating.

Having been in the States for ten days now (wow, that's gone fast), we feel qualified to make a couple of observations about key differences we've noticed, on this side of the pond.

The first is American toilet paper. Many years ago I had the dubious honour of working on the advertising account for Charmin bog rolls (a Proctor & Gamble trademark, I think I'm legally obliged to note). During the interminable meetings, the clients would make much play of their product's 'confidence factor'. I took this to mean that you could use it without worrying about the paper disintegrating and finding yourself wiping your arse with your bare hand. Well, the stuff we've encountered here - not just in remote roadside restrooms but in otherwise well-appointed hotels and restaurants - has a confidence factor of 1/10, at best. It would be perfect for playing a comb and paper. For its intended purpose, not so much. We may have to buy our own, once we reach a place that sells something more than souvenirs of the Blue Ridge Parkway.

The second is the bias of news media, which is scarcely believable to British sensibilities. There isn't even a pretence of journalistic balance or impartiality. Depending on which network or publication you favour, you'll either find Trump portrayed as a paragon of virtue and achievement, with his opponents accused of spreading fake news or being traitors. Or the orange one will be characterised as a buffoon, psychopath or criminal (often all three), and the pundits will be lining up to demand his immediate impeachment. Small wonder the great divide in American politics is showing no sign of narrowing.

Our neighbours for the night, in an inn perched high on an escarpment with miles of forests and other mountains spread out before it, were a couple from Georgia. They were sitting on the balcony when we ventured out to eat and, hearing our accents, dove straight in with questions about Brexit. We've already got used to this – it's our belief that Americans, of all persuasions, are relieved to know that another country is as polarised as theirs and as prone to eccentric decisions, so are eager to know more about us. We're quite happy to be clear about our position as Remainers and our belief that the referendum was ill-considered and gravely flawed, from start to finish, but we err on the side of caution when it comes to expressing opinions about their politics. We tread especially carefully when, like these folk, our new acquaintances have thick Southern accents. Perhaps unfairly we tend to associate the inhabitants of Dixie with 'Make America Great Again' bumper stickers and chants of "Build the wall", at rallies where dissenting voices are assaulted with impunity. But these two were lovely and wasted no time in expressing their distaste for Prima Donald.

A room with a view.

Song for the day: Dwight Yoakam – 'Waterfall'

This song, by one of country music's second generation of outlaws, isn't really about waterfalls. It's more Dwight's version of 'Imagine' or Mary Chapin Carpenter's 'In My Heaven'. But it fits with a day which reminded us that the best things in life often are free, despite what the Motown song might tell you to the contrary.
"My heart still believes that love
For what we need can be enough
If we'll just stop keepin' score."

Day 12 - HELLO DOLLY!

Blue Ridge Parkway → Sevierville TN

So goodbye Blue Ridge Parkway, hello Great Smoky Mountains. And, after savouring the prospect from the highest point on the Parkway at Richland Balsom (6047 ft), it was also goodbye sunshine, hello rain.

Perhaps surprisingly there was nothing to mark the end of the Parkway, after 469 memorable miles. No signs, no visitors centre, no rangers post. Just three elk – our first sighting of the trip – choosing the worst possible place to reach new grazing grounds, ambling across the intersection with the main highway and into a meadow on the other side. Fortunately for them the traffic, of which there was now quite an increase, was paying more heed than they were and they got across unscathed.

Elk mooning. (Not a sight we ever expected to see.)

The Smokies (as they're affectionately known) get their name from the whitish blue haze that often covers them. Hence also the Blue Ridge Mountains. And, for that matter, the Blue Mountains in Australia. I did find a detailed explanation of the photochemical process that creates this phenomenon, but I've always been hopeless at science and I glazed over after a couple of paragraphs. It was something to do with emanations from the vast profusion of plant life interacting with ozone particles. Anyway...

Great Soaky Mountains would have been a more appropriate name, on this particular day. After ninety minutes of driving alongside a fast filling creek, surrounded by dripping trees and cloud covered peaks, we were through the mountains and into Tennessee.

Truth be told, we were ready for a change. Even the most glorious landscapes and stunning views start to be taken for granted after five days. But maybe we weren't ready for the change we were about to encounter.

The instant we emerged from the woods and left the Smoky Mountains National Park, we were into Gatlinburg. Once a tiny hamlet, consisting of six houses, a blacksmith's, a general store and a church. Now a nightmare of neon - a ghastly array of fast food joints, shops selling 'crafts' of dubious authenticity and 'attractions' completely unrelated to those offered by Mother Nature. Ripley's Marvelous Mirror Maze & Candy Factory! The Salt & Pepper Shaker Museum! Gatlin's Laser Tag! Christ in the Smokies! (That last one is described as "The Nation's foremost Inspirational Attraction. Featuring incredibly realistic life-size scenes in the story of Christ utilizing life-size figures in dramatic settings.", but it could easily have been our reaction to what we were seeing.)

Suddenly we were in an endless line of cars, crawling from one stop light to the next. While the sidewalks overflowed with people who clearly only left their vehicles to waddle to the nearest eaterie or purveyor of mass-produced souvenirs. It wasn't only the weather that deterred us from disembarking.

Gatlinburg bills itself as 'The Gateway to The Smoky Mountains', but the huge disparity in visitor numbers, either side of the park border, suggested that only a small proportion actually venture beyond that border.

The trail of tat continued through Pigeon Forge, home to Dollywood, the ever-expanding theme park that pays profitable homage to East Tennessee's favourite daughter. Here the road was mostly lined with large hotels, where guests sat on their balconies, enjoying the view of the passing traffic and the other hotels opposite.

Dolly Parton was born and raised as one of twelve kids, in a tiny cabin on Locust Ridge, buried deep in the mountains we'd just come through. There's a picture of it on the cover of her 'My Tennessee Mountain Home' album and a replica of it at Dollywood, which I had absolutely no desire to see. We had briefly considered trying to find the real thing, but it's seriously off the beaten track at the end of a gravel road, which is apparently barricaded. I believe Dolly has bought the place and all the land around it to secure privacy.

Worshipping at the feet of greatness.

She did, however, attend high school in Sevierville. And then promptly left town the day after she graduated, which probably tells you something. Nevertheless, Sevierville has claimed her as its own, in a desperate (and, by the look of it, totally unsuccessful) bid to compete with the pulling power of its immediate neighbours. They've named a road after her and put a statue outside the county courthouse. The best you can say for it, is that it's a better likeness than the ridiculous effigy of Cristiano Ronaldo, which was displayed at his hometown in Madeira. It was deserted, as was the rest of the place.

After taking our souvenir photos and sending silent thanks to Dolly, for her magnificent music and inspiring life story, we went to look at the rest of downtown Sevierville. It didn't take long. We followed a Historic Walking Tour map, that we'd picked up at a gas station on the way in, which promised that what we were about to experience would be "really something special". Whoever wrote it needs to see a bit more of the world. Hardly any of the landmarks that it highlighted were more than a century old and none would get a second glance in a European town. Features deemed worth bragging about were the 13-inch thick walls of the courthouse and a house with three fireplaces (that fact even earned an exclamation mark). I know civic pride is something that should be encouraged, but come on…

On the plus side, though, it did give us an excuse to get out of the car and allowed us to rack up our 10,000 steps for the day.

What with the weather and the surroundings, we were feeling a bit sorry for ourselves when we arrived at our accommodation. And that, at first glance, did nothing to lift our spirits, being a chain motel indistinguishable from any other. Although, to be fair, our room was reasonably spacious and well kept. The only slightly unusual thing about it was an extra door at the far end, next to the bathroom. We assumed it was a cupboard, until we opened it and found ourselves stepping onto a small terrace area and gazing at a river.

This was the Little Pigeon River, the same waterway that runs near the old Parton family homestead. There were geese and ducks paddling by and, on the far bank, meadows with horses and wooded hills. Comparing it with a view of the highway, which is what most other hotel rooms in the vicinity seemed to have, we felt we were being smiled on again. We were even facing west, so a sunset beer beckoned.

Our mood improved even further when, overcome with indolence and a reluctance to endanger ourselves trying to cross any of the multiple lane freeways that surrounded us, we chose to eat at a restaurant called Shoney's, just a stone baked pizza's throw away from our hotel, on our side of the road. We'd never heard of Shoney's, but now know it's a franchised diner operation, operating mainly in the Southern states, with a familiar '50s heyday' style.

We were greeted like long-lost family by the guy at the door. The rest of the staff, whose figures bore ample testimony to the moreishness of their food, were every bit as friendly. While it was no-one's idea of *haute cuisine*, the buffet that was its centrepiece was both extensive and fresh… very different from the last time we'd been subjected to a buffet, at a time share resort in Turkey, which looked and smelt like something you'd hesitate to give to an animal (we never got as far as finding out what it tasted like). And the bill at the end of the evening was the lowest we've yet seen, even with the addition of the American-sized service charge that always seems preposterous to British eyes.

Song for the day: Dolly Parton – 'My Tennessee Mountain Home'

For once, the obvious choice is the correct choice. We've followed in Dolly's footsteps from the mountains of her childhood to the uninspiring surroundings of her academic years. Tomorrow we'll be tracing the next step of her journey to greatness, as we move on to Nashville. But however far Dolly has risen (and that's a very considerable distance) she always seems to have remained rooted in the memories and values of her formative experiences.

Day 13 - GUITAR TOWN

Sevierville → Nashville

We left the Gatlinburg/Pigeon Forge/Sevierville strip as we'd found it, in the rain. It felt as if the heavens were weeping over what Man had wrought below.

Driving through the foothills of the Smokies on such a day, passing by the remains of wooden cabins not dissimilar to the one which had housed the Parton family, it was obvious that Dolly's childhood must have been far from an uninterrupted rural idyll. So it's hardly surprising that, at the earliest opportunity, she was Nashville bound. As we were.

When we were planning our route across the country, Nashville took pride of place at the top of the 'to do' list. At least, for me. Tricia was happy to come along for the ride, in exchange for a *quid pro quo*, which we'll come to later. I've been a devotee of American roots music from the day an older cousin introduced me to Howlin' Wolf and Muddy Waters, before I was even into my teens. The discovery of country, via The Byrds, The Dillards and The Flying Burrito Brothers, soon followed and that was it. Ever since then, it only takes a long, lonesome note on a slide guitar or a rolling banjo lick and I'm hooked. Nashville may not be where that music originated, but it is now the spiritual and economic home.

I knew from watching the TV drama series of the same name, and reports from friends and relatives who had already been there, that Nashville has changed a lot in recent decades. It's been one of the fastest growing cities in the country, with a soaring population and rampant development, and it's become a major centre not just for the music business but for business of all kinds. Nevertheless, I was still eager to see it, at long last.

Before that though, as a farewell to Appalachian life, we took a short detour out of Sevierville and stopped off at Elvira's Café, on Wear Valley Road, which Trip Advisor told us was the best place for breakfast in the area. It was a Sunday morning and the whole county seemed to have the same idea. We did well to find both a parking space and a table. We'd anticipated a long-established country place, run by well-padded country matrons, but in fact the building was quite new and the owner was a Russian lady. What she was doing in this rural backwater is anyone's guess. The service and the food were exactly what we'd hoped for, though. Tricia pronounced their signature crepes to be first class and I was equally happy with my Country Ham & Eggs, once I'd asked them to hold the grits (if the name doesn't put you off this staple of Southern cuisine, the look of it will).

After a week of sticking to limits of 35mph on Skyline Drive and 45mph on the Blue Ridge Parkway, it was actually quite nice to be whisked through the rolling hills of East Tennessee at somewhat greater speed on today's journey of 200 miles. And necessary, as we had tickets for a show at the Ryman Auditorium in the evening, so couldn't hang about too much.

Nashville Skyline – 2019 version.

After dropping our bags at our B&B, we strolled across the Cumberland River towards a Nashville skyline that must be very different from what Dylan was thinking of. Corporate glass towers overwhelmed whatever remains of the more earthbound city, in both directions, and to our right were two more symbols of the new Nashville – the Nissan Stadium, home of the Tennessee Titans football team, and the Bridgestone Arena, home of the Nashville Predators ice hockey team. Having two teams playing at the highest national level, both in venues sponsored by Japanese companies, is as clear a sign of Nashville's change in status and circumstances as you're likely to find.

But sport isn't what brought us here. We could also identify Music Row - or Broadway, to give it the correct name – from the bridge over the river, as the sound was reaching us from several blocks away. Once there, it was deafening. Every bar (and there were countless numbers of them) had a live band going full tilt and open windows to give everyone in town a chance of hearing it. Add in the pedal taverns - mobile bars carrying up to a dozen heavy drinkers, which piped out their own music at great volume and rolled by at regular intervals – and the result was total cacophony. On the rare occasions when it was possible to identify a single source of sound among the maelstrom, it didn't sound good. But then it's hard to sing in tune, when you're struggling to hear yourself.

It was all a long way, a very long way, from the primarily acoustic music and the down home heartland values that I've always associated with Nashville. The hordes of inappropriately dressed and, even at 4 in the afternoon, mostly drunk visitors seemed to be enjoying it, however. Thank heavens, then, for the relative sanity of The Ryman, situated just off the main drag.

Seeing a show at the mother church of country music was one of the main missions of this trip and, having survived many threats and troubles over the years, the former tabernacle is a lovely venue which didn't disappoint.

For decades the Ryman was synonymous with The Grand Ole Opry, the live radio show that was instrumental in taking country music to the masses. When the Opry moved to its own bespoke, more spacious premises in 1974, there were plans to demolish the building and use the materials to construct a chapel at the new Opryland theme park. Thankfully those proposals, led by the owners of Opryland (cynically, some might think), were resisted and the Ryman was put on the National Register of Historic Places to protect it.

It fell into disuse for 20 years, however, before being restored during the 90s, both structurally and as a venue where people feel privileged to perform. It now has iconic status and, while country music continues to be at its heart, the stage hosts everything from stand-up comedy to rap groups.

With Bill Monroe – a stranger to Tricia.

We got there early, to soak up the atmosphere, and took photo opportunities with the statues of Bill Monroe and Little Jimmy Dickens outside the building, before going in. Bill Monroe, as the acknowledged father of bluegrass music, would seem an obvious choice for immortalisation. After all, he not only invented the genre in the 1940s, but the name was taken from his group, The Blue Grass Boys. Little Jimmy, maybe not so much. He was known for novelty songs, glitzy stage outfits and being a short arse, rather than any great musical innovation or achievement.

Once inside, we were able to admire how well the renovation had been done. When Emmylou Harris played here in 1991, before work began, no-one was allowed to sit on the balcony or beneath it, for fear it would collapse. The restoration has involved some significant changes to the building as a whole, mostly aimed at making things easier for both audience and performers. The old backstage facilities were dreadful, by all accounts, and the lack of air-conditioning could mean conditions were near intolerable in the warmer months. But the main auditorium has been kept as authentic as possible. They've even refurbished the old wooden pews. That doesn't make for the most comfortable of seating, but it does reflect the Ryman's original purpose as a place of worship. Which, in a way, it still is.

Going to church.

In an ideal world, we'd have been coming to see Dolly or Emmylou or Willie Nelson. What we actually had tickets for – in preference to Gladys Knight, Michelle Obama or Jon Anderson (former lead singer with Yes), who were the other acts appearing on days when we could have been in town, without completely throwing out our schedule – was a band called Midland. I'd never heard of them, but apparently they're quite successful. Certainly successful enough to fill the Ryman with a hugely enthusiastic and surprisingly mixed audience.

I'd persuaded Tricia to take an interest in the evening's proceedings by telling her that the three principals of Midland were quite handsome chaps, so she'd have something to look at, even if she wasn't too keen on what she was hearing. Her resentment was undisguised, therefore, when a bunch of guys, who could have been mistaken for short order cooks in a burger shack that was about to be closed down by the Food & Consumer Safety Bureau, wandered on. I had to reassure her that this was the support band, before she stalked out.

Midland were OK in a mainstream, Eaglesesque sort of way. On the downside, the percentage of random cover versions in the set indicated the thinness of their own catalogue; there was a bit too much self-congratulatory chat and preening - as you might expect from a band fronted by an actor/model; and, like the bands in the Music Row bars, volume and instrumentation were more rock than country. Bill Monroe and Little Jimmy would be turning in their graves.

Song for the day: Steve Earle – 'Guitar Town'

The title song from Steve's debut album is his homage to the town that would propel him to fame and then almost kill him. Three decades later and now a somewhat unlikely resident of New York City, he took the story full circle with 'Tennessee Blues' – "Won't be back no more, boys, won't see me around, Goodbye guitar town."

Day 14 - NASHVILLE CATS

Nashville

After spending yesterday sampling what 'new' country has to offer, today was devoted to the real deal. First stop was the Country Music Hall of Fame & Museum. The Walk of Fame in the park outside had some strange inclusions – Peter Frampton? Steve Winwood? But no Merle Haggard or Patsy Cline or Charley Pride? What are the criteria for earning a star here? Thankfully, they'd got it spot on inside the museum.

Right at the start of the tour was a splendid Emmylou Harris exhibition. I hadn't known about this and was thrilled. For a brief period, in the mid-70s, I had made a modest living, met a lot of interesting people and indulged in an indecent amount of misbehaviour as a music journalist. Emmylou was the first artist I ever interviewed.

As a newbie, I was a bit nervous. As someone unused to running the press gauntlet, at the time, so was she. After exchanging tentative pleasantries, I asked an opening question and she gushed non-stop for the whole allotted hour, answering most of my other questions in the process. She's held a special place in my heart ever since. She's also gone on to have an award-studded career as one of contemporary country's music most pioneering and respected figures, and the museum did her full justice.

The day after I interviewed Emmylou, Tricia and I had gone to see her play in London with The Hot Band – a combo including several members of Elvis Presley's backing band, who more than lived up to their name. The music was wonderful, but what particularly impressed Tricia were the knee-high, oxblood red leather boots that Emmylou was wearing. For years afterwards she tried to find a pair for herself, but never saw their like again… until now. The same boots were the first item on display in the exhibition.

Elsewhere it was good to see some of country music's dusty side roads – such as the Texas scene and the so-called Outlaw movement, led by Waylon Jennings and Willie Nelson – given plenty of mileage. Guy Clark, a leading light among the Texas coterie and another special favourite of mine, appeared way more than I'd expected.

Halfway round we came to The Rotunda, an extensive circular chamber containing a multitude of plaques with 3D bronze portraits of selected Hall of Fame inductees. As with Madame Tussauds waxworks, some of these likenesses were pretty good, while others were a bit weird. Elvis had been portrayed as if he'd suffered a stroke, for example, while Waylon looked more like a Grecian 2000 model than an outlaw.

We (meaning I) eventually had to tear ourselves away from the Hall of Fame, because we (again meaning I) also wanted to get to the Johnny Cash Museum. Producer Rick Rubin resuscitated Johnny's career in his latter years, so he went out on a high, and the Cash family have done a great job of nurturing his legacy and legend. The Man In Black has become a towering figure, not just in music but in American culture. The museum was a moving testament to who he was, what he did and what he suffered for his art.

In the presence of greatness, yet again.

Both of these collections were outstandingly well curated and presented. Tricia might not like the idea, but our entire time in Nashville could have been spent in those two museums, without coming close to seeing and hearing everything on show. The Hall of Fame owns hundreds of thousands of sound recordings, photos and films, thousands of costumes, hundreds of instruments linked to noted country artists and countless other pieces of memorabilia, only a fraction of which can exhibited at any one time. We're already thinking of another American road trip, at some point in the future, taking in parts of the Deep South that we won't be seeing this time around. It may need to incorporate Nashville again. But please don't let Tricia know that.

After communing with the spirits of country music icons, we were ready for a live taste of what it's all about. The lady running our B&B was also a musician (isn't everybody in this town?), so we'd asked her for a suggestion. Without hesitation, she recommended seeing a band called The Time Jumpers, who play every Monday night at 3rd and Lindsley, a large bar some way off the main drag. She'd said we should book tickets in advance, as they always sell out, and get there early. Fortunately we did both, because every table in the house was taken, well over an hour before show time.

On the way in, the ticket lady was asking everyone to share their tables, if they had spare seats. We had two free, when we first sat down, and it stayed like that for some time, despite our location being a choice one, on the balcony just above the stage. It was probably because a lot of people were arriving in larger groups. Or maybe no-one liked the look of us. Either way, eventually a pleasant couple came along and asked if they could fill the gaps. It transpired they weren't actually a couple but work colleagues from a geeky new age operation in San Francisco, who'd come to Nashville for a conference or seminar or techy tradeshow, or some such. They did give us an enthusiastic explanation of what their business was all about and why it was going to be a sensational success, but the surrounding noise and our almost complete ignorance of such matters made it difficult to understand. We were on better ground when we moved on to talking about music and what we were up to on our odyssey. They also gave us a full rundown on things to do and places to go, when we finally reach the

Golden Gate City. Few of which we'll be able to remember, in all likelihood, as we weren't taking notes.

Their company made a fine evening even more enjoyable and, just to put a cherry on it, after they'd departed as soon as the band finished and we asked to settle our bill, the waitress told us that all the drinks had already been paid for. We wished that we'd had a chance to thank them – or rather to thank whoever signs off their expense account – and that we'd drunk a lot more.

The Time Jumpers were an assembly of veteran session guys - drums, double bass, three fiddles, two guitars, pedal steel and a piano/accordion player. They did two sets of country, bluegrass and western swing songs and instrumentals, with a smattering of gospel and blues thrown in, as guest vocalists got up to join them. All delivered with consummate musicianship and effortless interplay.

The sound balance was brilliant too. You could hear every note being played by every instrument, not one of which was duff. The guys pounding away in the Music Row bars – and the gentlemen of Midland, come to that – should drop by for a masterclass.

How it should be done - The Time Jumpers in full swing.

At the end of the evening, we asked one of the barmaids to call a cab to take us home, as our landlady had advised. It wasn't a great distance back to base, but it would have taken us through an area of town that was probably not best ventured into by a couple of middle-aged honkies, in the late hours of the night.

We went outside the bar to wait. And we waited. And we waited. Vehicles came and went, and the other audience members gradually dispersed. Then the staff started leaving. Eventually, the chap who either ran or owned the place emerged and locked up. We explained our dilemma and he reckoned that our ride had been pilfered – whether knowingly or not – by someone else in need of a cab. He asked where we were going and, bless his heart, gave us a lift to our front door. Great bar, great band, great people. If you could award a place more than 5 stars on Trip Advisor, we would unhesitatingly give them to 3rd and Lindsley.

Our bedroom at the B&B, by the way, was one of the more interesting ones we've slept in thus far. Called The Music City Room, it had a bath and shower right next to the bed, surrounded by a curtain decorated with staves and notes. The rest of the room was decorated with assorted posters, photos and magazine covers, celebrating the full range of country singers, from Don Williams to Miranda Lambert. And on the bed itself lay a cushion carrying the likeness of Mr Cash. There was no danger of not knowing where we were, when we woke up.

Song for the day: Lovin' Spoonful – 'Nashville Cats'

There have been many songs written about this town, from The Delmore Brothers' 'Nashville Blues' to The Foo Fighters' 'Congregation'. But after witnessing The Time Jumpers, this is the one that sprang to mind. "Play clean as country water"? They sure did.

Day 15 – GOING DOWN TO MISSISSIPPI

Nashville → Belmont MS

Unlike the Aussies, who seemed intent on eradicating all trace of their murky origins, our cousins on this side of the pond are good at preserving and/or restoring their past… what there is of it. Even if that sometimes requires a bit of a stretch, as we saw a few days ago. The pitiful 'historic district' of Sevierville consisted of half a dozen buildings, scattered around the desolate centre of the town, most of which were erected in the 1940s and showed no sign of their original purpose.

On the way out of Nashville we stopped off at Belle Meade, a plantation site where the owners had built a large fortune and a substantial antebellum mansion on the sweat of others' brows. John Harding, the man who started with a smallish farm in 1806 and developed it into a great estate, ended up as one of the biggest slave holders in the Nashville area. More admirably, he also became a very successful horse breeder. Although any favourable impression was soon dispelled by an information board showing a copy of a notice he'd issued, offering a $20 reward for the return of a runaway slave named Ben – described as "tolerably black".

The property changed hands several times, during the first half of the 20th century, and its glory faded through a succession of financial setbacks. It was finally bought by the State of Tennessee in 1953 and handed over to the Association for the Preservation of Tennessee Antiquities, to ensure its survival. It has, of course, been turned into a tourist attraction, complete with restaurant, gift shop, guided tours, wine and bourbon tastings, and event hosting. And, unlike some of the other publicly-owned attractions that we've visited, it's not free. We weren't intending to stay long, so when we realised that entry tickets were priced at $24 or more – not even for everything, but for each different element of the place – we turned to leave. As this was the same as what we'd paid for admission to the whole of the Country Music Hall of Fame Museum, it felt like a rip-off. We're happy to contribute to local economies when we're travelling, but there are limits.

How a slave owner lived.

On our return to the car, however, we spotted a pathway leading from the other side of the car park to an old cabin, standing alone among magnificent trees. This was the Harding Cabin – the rather more modest home that John Harding built for his family, when they first came here. Later, when they moved on to better things, it was lived in for many years by Robert 'Uncle Bob' Green, one of the estate's slaves who stayed after emancipation to be a key part of the horse breeding programme. When President Grover Cleveland visited Belle Meade, in 1887, The New York Times reported: "The President has made the personal acquaintance of Uncle Bob. Every stockman in the country knows of Uncle Bob, the colored major domo of the Belle Meade stock farm and one of the chief authorities on blooded stock in the world."

Leaving the cabin, the path continued on through the grounds, to reach what appeared to be the frontage of the main house, a handsome neo-Grecian mansion. We followed it and soon found ourselves doing a full circuit of the gardens and the exterior of the buildings, spending more time than we'd planned, without it costing a cent. Score one to the Brits. This may have been our first victory in Tennessee since the War of 1812.

The Natchez Trace Parkway, on which we spent the rest of the day travelling south out of Tennessee, across the northwest corner of Alabama and into Mississippi, was another chapter in 'The Most Scenic Drives In

America'. Like the Blue Ridge, it's a parkway in the intended sense, extending some 450 miles along the line of an ancient track, used to transport goods and fighting men since long before the white settlers arrived. While it lacked the stunning vistas of the Appalachians, it was rich in stories and sites of note. As well as some lovely waterfalls.

Far less grand than Belle Meade, but arguably with as good a tale to tell, was the Gordon House, one of the few buildings on the Natchez Trace that date back to the old pathway. It wasn't much to look at – a squat, plain two storey dwelling in a basic Georgian style. But it had belonged to a Captain John Gordon, who ran a ferry across the nearby Duck River. Permission to operate the service was granted by Chief George 'Tootemastubbe' Colbert, leader of the local Chickasaw people who still held sway here at the time. Colbert had his own ferry, on the much larger Tennessee River to the north.

How a ferry owner lived.

Both men were associates of future president General Andrew Jackson, during his numerous campaigns against the British and the native tribes, and both provided the General with use of their ferries to move his army about. Chief George must have been the smarter businessman of the two, however. He reportedly charged Jackson $75,000 (around $1.5m today) to help bring his men home after the Battle of New Orleans in 1815. Judging by his house, John Gordon never made that sort of money. He built it after retiring from the military and died from pneumonia within a year of finishing the job.

Andrew Jackson's name cropped up again soon afterwards, when we reached Jackson Falls, an attractive cascade in a heavily wooded section of the afore-mentioned Duck River. The trail down from the car park was described as 'steep'. It certainly wasn't flat, and it was slightly slippery in places after recent rain, but 'steep' was yet another park service exaggeration and we were soon standing alongside the water, taking souvenir photos.

Jackson Falls – just before fleeing from the chiggers.

The pools beneath the falls looked as if they would have been a perfect spot for a refreshing dip, at the height of summer. Until another couple, who were there at the same time, told us about the dreaded Tennessee

Chiggers. These, apparently, are minute larvae – so small as to be almost invisible – capable of causing discomfort that's completely out of proportion to their size. Once they've leapt from a nearby leaf or blade of grass onto you (they favour moist areas of the body, we were informed) they burrow into your pores and feed on skin cells, until they get bored and hop off again. The result is an unsightly rash, plus itching that can drive you mad and last up to two weeks.

The couple we met were particularly concerned about our lack of awareness re the danger we were facing, a) because this sort of place, near water and with plentiful vegetation, is Shangri-la for chiggers and b) we were both wearing short-sleeved shirts, making us prime targets for the little buggers. The couple made us feel that hazmat suits would have been the only attire fit for the occasion, and handed over a bottle of tick repellent, insisting we apply it liberally. Which we did, before evacuating the area with almost unseemly speed. Tricia still has nightmares about her encounter with leeches, in the tropical rainforests of Australia, and didn't want to risk another insect attack.

Having recently read a book about the Lewis & Clark expedition, which was instrumental in opening up the western half of America in the early years of the 19th century, I was particularly interested to come across the matter-of-factly named Meriwether Lewis Death and Burial Site. On returning from that epic, three year voyage of exploration, Lewis had been on his way from Louisiana to Washington, to sort out issues over the cost of the enterprise, when he stopped off at Grinder's Stand, a small inn next to the Natchez Trace track. During the night he died of gunshot wounds. These were said at the time to be self-inflicted – Lewis seems to have been a complex and mercurial character – but suspicions of murder have persisted ever since.

Either way, his passing has been commemorated with an informative site, including a surviving stretch of the path on which he originally travelled through the woods, and a solid (if less than beautiful) monument, erected over his grave.

Our destination for the night was the tiny town of Belmont, just off the Parkway. First impressions were of what Jack would call a bumtown - a place that looked to be completely devoid of life and hope. Even inhabitants. Then we discovered a country store/post office/gas station selling top notch ice cream, along with fishing bait, ice bags, chewing tobacco and all the other essentials of rural life in Mississippi.

Even better was The Belmont Historic Hotel, which was an absolute delight. It was built in 1924, which again may raise European eyebrows at the use of the word 'historic', but it was a genuine step back in time, being decorated and furnished like a 19th century English country house. The cast of Downton Abbey would have fitted in very nicely. And it's run by a very sweet lady, who welcomed us in true Southern style. A style which was continued by the wraparound porch, complete with rocking chair, where I administered my first cold beer of the evening.

Song for the day: ZZ Top – 'My Head's In Mississippi'

ZZ Top are, of course, that little ol' band from Texas. But the blues-based music that Billy Gibbons and his buddies have helped bring into the 21st century hails from these parts. We'll be exploring those roots over the coming days. Meanwhile, this will set us up nicely.

Day 16 - DIFFERENT ROADS

Belmont MS → Memphis

Based on the evidence accumulated thus far, it would appear that your chances of achieving musical greatness are much improved, if you've been brought up dirt poor. After going back to the roots of Dolly and Johnny, with their large families in tiny cabins, it was the turn of Elvis, with his not so large family but still in a tiny cabin.

First, though, we had to say a sad farewell to the Natchez Trace Parkway, which had enchanted us for the previous 24 hours. From talking with a park ranger, we found out that it changes significantly over the remaining 250 miles to the south, which we weren't going to see. Swamps and alligators would have awaited us, rather than farmlands and countless oak trees. That'll be another one for the bucket list, when we visit New Orleans on a future trip.

We made a couple of quick stops before turning off. Pharr Mounds is a site featuring eight Indian burial mounds, randomly scattered over a huge meadow. These grassy bumps range in size from the height of a giraffe to the height of a toddler, and are up to fifty or sixty metres in length. Stonehenge, The Great Pyramids or the Parthenon, they're not. But they're estimated to be around two thousand years old – so genuine antiquities, especially by American standards – they're a treasure trove for archaeologists and, as with other ancient constructions, they're impressive for the effort and ingenuity that must have gone into them, given the minimal technology available to their creators.

More affecting, even though far more recent, were the Graves of the Unknown Soldiers. This was a bosky spot on another surviving part of the old pathway, where thirteen Confederate soldiers had been buried, either during or after the Civil War. No-one knows who they were or how they died – no battles were fought anywhere near here – and speculation ranges from their being victims of disease, which accounted for vast numbers of combatants over the course of the war, to meeting their fate as they tried to make their way home once the Confederacy had surrendered. Many on the losing side perished in the aftermath, either from starvation or at the hands of renegade Unionists, out for revenge. Thirteen headstones were finally put in place by the side of the path, in 1940, only to be stolen and then replaced by the National Park Service. They're now decorated with American and Confederate flags, and a variety of tributes from visitors. Disturbed only by birdsong and the rustling of leaves, the nameless fallen are genuinely resting in peace.

What was once the busiest road for miles around.

From anonymity to the pinnacle of fame. Tupelo is a town (or city, as they insist on calling them here) with a population of less than 40,000 and no distinguishing features. It would almost certainly go unnoticed by the outside world, were it not responsible for giving that world the gift of one Elvis Aaron Presley.

The Elvis Presley Birthplace was signposted from miles away. Yet once we got there it was, again, surprisingly quiet. The lady who greeted us effusively at the ticket desk said we'd been fortunate in avoiding the arrival of coach parties shipped in from Memphis. We couldn't imagine we would have him to ourselves when we got to Graceland.

We'd expected to spend maybe an hour at the Birthplace, but were there way longer than that. The two-roomed cabin where he was born, restored and refurnished but still in its original location, is just the centrepiece of a multi-faceted set-up. The city bought the home and a wide area of land around it, using a donation from Elvis in 1957, and the attraction now includes the church where the family worshipped – brought in from another site and reconstructed – a museum, a theatre, a chapel of remembrance, gardens with statues of the younger and older Elvis, and (naturally) a gift shop.

From humble beginnings…

The church, a humble wooden affair not much bigger than the cabin, offered a presentation about church life when the Presleys were among the congregation. In all the pictures we were shown, there was not a single non-white face to be seen. Wherever it was that Elvis absorbed the black music, which would be such a crucial element in his revolutionary stylistic hybrid, it wasn't here.

The museum had a range of artifacts, photos and audiovisual stuff, painting a picture of the great man's upbringing. And the Story Wall, on the outside of the main building, carried testimonies and reflections from boyhood friends, family members and others who knew him back then,

The most enlightening part of our tour, however, was a chat with the lady looking after the cabin itself. Despite having built it themselves, the family had been kicked out of this place when Elvis was three years old, after his dad defaulted on the repayments and was jailed for forging a cheque. They then had eight more homes in Tupelo, before moving to Memphis when he was 13. According to our informant, there was no good reason why the Presley family should have suffered such hard times before Elvis transformed their fortunes. She was unequivocal in her assessment of why things weren't better for them - "Vernon was just too damn lazy to work", she said. (He outlived his son, of course, so maybe indolence has something to recommend it.)

The impression given by the Birthplace was of a happy childhood, despite the disruptions and deprivations, and of a very amiable, well brought-up young man, who only got into music by accident – he was given an $8 guitar for his eleventh birthday, when his mum refused to let him have a gun or a bicycle, as they would have been too dangerous. We'll no doubt learn more about his transition from there to fat boy on the bog, during the next leg of the journey.

The Presleys had fled from Tupelo to Memphis in a green Plymouth sedan. Seventy years later we followed them in our Nissan saloon. Although this is obviously far less characterful, it does have the great advantages of being waterproof and having our satnav on board. Which proved to be an absolute boon, as we arrived in rush hour Memphis at the same time as driving rain. Heaven knows how long it would have taken to find our hotel without it.

A short distance down the road from the hotel was a restaurant called The Bar-B-Q Shop. It claimed to be 'world famous' and offer 'the #1 ribs in America'. We'd never heard of it and the extravagant boast was, of course, impossible to put to the test. But we were starving and the prospect of top-notch ribs was irresistible.

We've already had that all-American favourite a couple of times since arriving Stateside, and many times on previous trips, so we knew that ribs here are a different proposition to what we'd get back home. Perhaps because of an alternative approach to butchering, American ribs tend to be far meatier than their British equivalent. The portions, as you would expect, are far bigger (what we ended up with looked like half an animal, minus its head and tail). And the options are bewildering – it's not just a question of a whole rack or half.

We spent some time studying the menu. Should we go for pork or beef? Slab or tips? Wet, dry or glazed? Mild or hot? It was a lot to think about, at the end of a long day. Eventually the waitress came to our rescue and suggested that one of us order pork and one beef, and that we both go for the half and half option, when it came to the BBQ coatings. Then we could share and get a taste of almost everything. We were only too happy to take her advice.

We couldn't possibly say which of the variations was best – they all went down very well. Interestingly, they came accompanied by something called Texas Toast. (Sorry, "our famous Texas Toast".) This was basically a variation on garlic bread, using thick white slices rather than baguettes. It was OK, and a nice change from the ubiquitous fries, but certainly not the highlight of the meal.

If we'd been really intent on staying true to our pursuit of Elvis, we'd have looked for somewhere offering peanut butter, banana and bacon sandwiches. But they sound pretty revolting and we were quite relieved they weren't on the otherwise extensive Bar-B-Q shop menu.

Song for the day: Elvis Presley – 'Don't Cry Daddy'

Gladys, Elvis's mum, was the most important person in his life and her early death seems to have been a blow from which he never really recovered. As an only child (his twin brother, Jesse, died at birth) he was smothered with love and care, that sought to make up for the material things that his upbringing lacked. Seeing his birthplace was a reminder of what he wanted to rise above, taking his parents with him. Tomorrow we'll see just how well he succeeded in that ambition.

Day 17 – GRACELAND AND BEYOND

Memphis

Today was all about more musical pilgrimages. First to the King's palace, and then to the less opulent source of some of his inspiration.

Our visit to Graceland got off to a good start. The obvious place to leave your car is in the official parking lot, at a cost of $10. Or you could go a little further to a shopping mall, where it would be free, though that wasn't recommended for safety reasons. (It may have been a pleasant neighbourhood, back in the 50s, but these days the Whitehaven district isn't the most sought-after area of Memphis.) We found a third, even better alternative. On arriving at the entrance we spotted a lay-by, right outside the front wall of the mansion itself and directly across the road from the rest of the Presley theme park. A few other vehicles were there already, but space was available, there were no visible restrictions and the guards at the gates of Graceland were only yards away. It couldn't have been more convenient or more secure. Or any cheaper.

It's often been noted that The King's gaff is smaller than you might expect, and it is. In fact seeing the interior of the mansion was the least enjoyable bit of the whole experience. Only a few of the rooms on the ground floor and the low-ceilinged basement, which housed Elvis's play areas, are open to the public. Shuffling round them, being jostled by visitors competing for photo space, felt quite claustrophobic, and things were made worse by the interactive iPad guided tour, which every visitor was given. Mine seemed to have a mind of its own. It was supposed to move on from one room or section to the next, along with you, at the touch of a button. But mine kept freezing, going back to the start or skipping to another part of the place. I'm sure our sons would say it was the fault of their Luddite father, being all fingers and thumbs with any technology more recent than 1980. I would say that, if this stuff is supposed to be intuitive and idiot-proof, then clearly it isn't as advertised.

The house must have been crowded back in the day, too. Elvis always shared it with his parents, his grandmother and the gaggle of the good ol' boys known as The Memphis Mafia. His wife and daughter joined them for a few years, and then his girlfriend.

The house was redecorated several times over the two decades before Elvis died. Starting with his mother's simple taste, as shown by her bedroom on the ground floor, and proceeding to the cavalcade of kitsch that dominates everywhere else.

I have reason to believe we both will be received in Graceland.

Anyway… once through the labyrinth of the house and into the gardens and the outhouses, things got a lot less hectic and much better. We saw the racquetball court, which was part of the Presley exercise routine, during his fit years; the office from which his dad tried to look after his son's personal finances (a losing battle, one would imagine, given Elvis's cavalier approach to money and possessions) and the management of the estate; and, most interestingly, the Trophy Building – a seemingly inappropriate but possibly revealing name for a space that contained a wealth of memorabilia relating to his life at Graceland, with particular emphasis on the period when he shared it with Priscilla and his daughter, Lisa Marie, who now owns the joint.

Last, but by no means least, was the Meditation Garden, where Elvis has been laid to rest, along with his parents, his grandma and his stillborn twin brother. The air of melancholy that hung over this spot seemed to us to sum up the whole place. This was not, however, a sentiment shared by most of our fellow visitors, as they excitedly took turns to immortalise themselves posing in front of the graves.

The mansion and its grounds are now just a small part of a massive 'entertainment complex', which includes exhibits of Elvis's cars, planes and other boy's toys, as well as a multi-roomed museum, a theatre and The Guesthouse, a sprawling resort hotel next door. While the man's talent, charisma and influence naturally get priority, much play is also made of his undoubted generosity and charitable giving, and his supposedly flawless character. His two years in the army get a huge room to themselves, as evidence of his allegedly unspoiled nature. Even though the reality of his service experience is that he was allowed to live off-base with his family, while in Germany, and seems to have spent a fair bit of his time there either partying or developing the drug addiction that would eventually kill him.

Noticeable by their absence - both visually and narratively - are any mentions whatsoever of the malign presence of Colonel Tom or the tragic decline into obesity and pharmaceuticals. If you want the unvarnished truth about Elvis's life, there are plenty of documentaries and books on the subject.

For all their efforts to create an airbrushed legacy, the abiding impression from our visit was of a life that delivered great rewards and hopefully some great satisfactions, but was never really his own. We'll leave the final word to Dolly Parton, one of the contributors to the Icons exhibit, in which stars who followed on from Elvis bear testimony to his importance – "If your actions create a legacy that inspires others to dream more, learn more, do more and become more, then you have accomplished something. Elvis did that and more, for me and for so many others."

After leaving Graceland there was time for a quick photo op at Sun Studio, where Elvis was discovered and made his earth-shaking early recordings, before heading to Beale Street and the Mississippi River.

Even 400 miles upstream from the Gulf, the Mississippi earns its nickname of 'The Big Muddy'. It's indisputably big and you wouldn't want to swim in it... not here, anyway. But the paddle boats at anchor by the jetties, protruding at regular intervals along the banks, made a fine sight.

Between the wars, Beale Street was a thriving hub of the black community and a musical mecca. All the great jazz and blues artists of the era came through. BB King, among others, made his name here and is commercially commemorated with a club and a gift shop. Memphis Blues became yet another sub-genre. By the 60s, however, the area had fallen into disuse and disrepair, before being restored as a tourist magnet in the 80s and 90s. Joining the throng, we stopped off at A. Schwab's Soda Fountain – an establishment that's survived the ups and downs of Beale Street since 1876 –and enjoyed an iced coffee at a pavement table, while watching the world go by and listening to a live facsimile of the music that made this place famous, wafting from a band in the bar across the street.

Here's to Beale Street and the music it's given us.

Between the wars, Beale Street was a thriving hub of the black community and a musical mecca. All the great jazz and blues artists of the era came through. BB King, among others, made his name here and is commercially commemorated with a club and a gift shop. Memphis Blues became yet another sub-genre. By the 60s, however, the area had fallen into disuse and disrepair, before being restored as a tourist magnet in the 80s and 90s. Joining the throng, we stopped off at A. Schwab's Soda Fountain – an establishment that's survived the ups and downs of Beale Street since 1876 –and enjoyed an iced coffee at a pavement table, while watching the world go by and listening to a live facsimile of the music that made this place famous, wafting from a band in the bar across the street.

Like Sunset Strip in LA and Music Row in Nashville, Beale Street now consists almost entirely of bars, restaurants and souvenir shops, most of them with no semblance of the authenticity that A. Schwab's can claim. But here the visitor-friendly amenities come with a big side order of seediness. Begging seemed to be a local pastime and WC Handy Park, right next to the main drag, hosted a whole bunch of people you wouldn't want to meet in a dark alley, to go with a statue of the great man. We decided that lingering after nightfall was likely to be dodgy at best and dangerous at worst, so went elsewhere to eat.

That proved to be a very good call. Having been steered towards the #1 ribs in America at The Bar-B-Q Store last night, we put our trust in recommendations again. They pointed us to Huey's - a long standing Memphis institution, also on the same street as our hotel, which has been voted as having the best burgers in town every year since 1984.

The place was buzzing, with a lively young crowd and music that matched the nostalgic vibe of the place. The walls were covered with music and Americana related memorabilia, and the tables with red and white checked cloths. From what we could see at other tables, everyone was having the burgers, which were towering affairs that needed to be held together by a skewer. Eating them while retaining dignity and not requiring laundry services was going to be a challenge.

Before getting that far, we had to negotiate yet another menu of bewildering complexity. The basic Huey Burger ('world famous', we weren't surprised to be told) was pretty much your standard combo of ingredients and just one of a dozen variations on the burger theme. Plus a DIY option, choosing from a long list of possible additions, if none of the fixed options were quite right. And that was before we even got round to considering the pages of sandwiches, salads, seafood baskets, wraps and other delights that were on offer.

It had to be burgers, though – the world famous one for Tricia, and the even more hard-to-handle 'Old Tyme A1' for me, complete with bacon, onion, mushrooms and three different cheeses. Were they the best in town? Not having sampled all the burgers in Memphis, we can't possibly confirm or dispute this accolade. But they were bloody good and are highly recommended, should you ever find yourself in these parts.

Song for the day: Gillian Welch – 'Elvis Presley Blues'

The obvious choice would have been Paul Simon's 'Graceland', but this gets to the heart of how we felt, having traced the Elvis saga from birthplace to final resting place. "He was all alone in a long decline"… sadly, that pretty much sums it up.

Day 18 - DOWN TO THE CROSSROADS

Memphis → Clarksdale MS

After a few days in the hurly burly of Nashville and Memphis, the next couple of weeks will be taking us into the less populous heartland of America. A section of the journey that should show us aspects of the country and landscapes that we've never seen before, and which we're particularly looking forward to.

Highway 61 - the most iconic road in America after Route 66, thanks to the Bob Dylan album title and the numerous songs written about it – takes travellers from Minnesota right down to New Orleans, and vice versa. During the middle 1900s, it was one of the main conduits of the Great Migration – the movement of millions of black folk, fleeing the racism and poverty of the rural South, in search of more remunerative work and a better life in the industrialised North.

In the more southerly part of its journey, which is what we'll be tracing, it's touted as The Blues Highway – a classification that's been eagerly taken up by local tourist boards and chambers of commerce – owing to its connection with the early years of blues music and musicians, many of whom ended up being part of that migration. Muddy Waters, for example, was born and raised in Mississippi as McKinley Morganfield. He started his career playing acoustic blues in the Delta style, before moving to Chicago at the age of 30, changing his name, forming a band and becoming a prime mover of the urban, electric blues genre.

The highway is also known as The Great River Road, since it follows the course of the Mississippi for most of the way. But in the eighty miles from Memphis to Clarksdale, we didn't get a single glimpse of the legendary river. We did see a lot of water, however. Much of the very flat land, which stretched away into the distance on either side of the road, was flooded to some extent. And once we reached Clarksdale, the rains came down and didn't stop for the rest of the day.

We scheduled this trip for late April through to early June, because all the meteorological data pointed to this being the ideal period for doing the whole thing, across the full range of climate zones, in conditions that would vary from pleasant to reach-for-the-sunblock. With minimal risk of extreme weather events, apart from the remote possibility of meeting up with a twister while crossing Tornado Alley – the belt that runs through the Great Plains from the Canadian border down to Texas, and which is usually most active during the late spring months.

It isn't working out quite as planned. From the moment we arrived, the weather has defied predictions, in all sorts of ways and in pretty much all parts. Our brief 'all seasons in three days' stay in New York was a taste of things to come and of what the rest of the country has been getting. Georgia and Alabama are clocking up record highs. The northern states are still in winter. The West Coast has been unusually cool. And huge areas of the Mid West are being hit by torrential storms. We've dodged the worst till now, but the news channels have been getting very excited about it.

Fortunately our main business of the day has involved being indoors. Almost all the most significant names in the history of the blues, from Leadbelly and Charley Patton to Elmore James and Muddy, were born somewhere near this stretch of road. And they all get recognition at the Gateway to the Blues Museum in Tunica and the Delta Blues Museum in Clarksdale.

The first museum of the day.

The Tunica place has been created in a splendidly atmospheric disused railway depot. Some of the old track still runs outside it. It had some interesting exhibits about the origins of the blues in these parts and a wealth of artwork, depicting both blues artists across the decades and life along the Mississippi.

The one in Clarksdale is more extensive and more celebrated. It's an excellent museum at a very reasonable price (just $8 for oldies). The archive videos of artists both known and unknown were particularly good, and we spent the afternoon engaging with yet more stories of journeys from poverty to prominence, while being serenaded by the music.

What was it about this music, linked directly to the black slave experience, that resonated so strongly with white teenagers in the Home Counties of England, during the early '60s? The so-called 'British Blues Boom' produced seminal bands, such as The Stones and The Yardbirds, and a whole dressing roomful of guitar heroes, from Eric Clapton to Jimmy Page. It also established the template for most rock bands ever since, and inspired a renaissance of homegrown blues in America, at a time when it was being largely ignored by black audiences, in favour of soul.

One can only imagine that the feelings of frustration and lack of freedom, which the great blues artists so powerfully express, struck a chord with the young in a repressed and deprived post-WWII Britain. I still remember hearing John Lee Hooker for the first time, at an older cousin's house, when I was about eleven years old. The music, though primitive in some respects, had a passion and a depth that clearly differentiated it from the frothy pop that the BBC (the only radio option available in the UK, at the time) was putting out in very limited quantities. Even at that early age, I think I recognised that this was music made by men, not boys. My own musical path was set, from that moment

The Oscar-winning screenwriter, William Goldman, talked about the divide between what he called 'comic book movies' and 'non-comic book movies'… those whose primary motivation is to be part of the commercial mainstream, to match popular expectation and to entertain; and those coming from a more personal place, delving into less predictable and often darker territory. Surprisingly, yet persuasively, he cites 'The Deer Hunter' as an example of the former and 'Bambi' as an example of the latter. The same distinction could be applied to music, and there's no doubt where my heart lies.

Once outside the museum, downtown Clarksdale looked like a war zone, especially in the rain, with almost every building in an advanced state of disrepair. But, in some cases, this outward appearance disguises a business riding on the town's increasing tourist appeal and seeking to establish some sort of authenticity. Morgan Freeman's Ground Zero Blues Club, for instance, which at first glance looked to be abandoned and derelict. It was shut at the back end of the afternoon, but we spoke with a lady who was tidying up on the veranda by the front door. She told us they'd be open for the evening and they didn't take bookings – we got the impression that this common practice was disdained as being too conventional and, indeed, too organised for such a wild and woolly place.

Got those run down, pouring down, get out of town Clarksdale blues.

The joint was already jumping when we got back there for the evening, around 7.30. (Again, where do all these people come from? During the daylight hours, Clarksdale appeared to be a town that had been evacuated.) Nevertheless, we managed to find space at a table with a nice couple from up state Mississippi. We settled down to enjoy some food and music, which they assured us would be good as "no-one jest wolks in offa the street and plays heeyar".

The food - fried chicken and a pulled pork sandwich - was fine. The music, maybe not so much. The large lady fronting the band was entertaining, in a crazed Jerry Lee Lewis channelling kind of way and was certainly passionate about what she was doing. The rest of the musicians, however, seemed to be unacquainted with each other and even, at times, with their instruments.

Away from the stage, the décor and the clientele were entertainment enough. The walls and ceiling were covered with musical instruments, flags, posters, portraits of old bluesmen and graffiti, all made to look as if they had been randomly thrown together without a moment's thought. We cynically guessed that, in reality, it was the carefully considered work of a big city design agency, which had cost Mr Freeman and his partners a fortune.

Song for the day: Robert Johnson – 'Cross Road Blues'

There are several places that claim to be the setting for Robert Johnson's mythical, career-transforming encounter with the Devil, but Clarksdale is the one that has the biggest marker and is making the most capital out of the connection. The look and vibe of the place – partly the result of decades of neglect and decline, but increasingly the product of savvy 'preservation' – match the legend perfectly.

Day 19 - HIGH WATER EVERYWHERE

Clarksdale

Our accommodation in Clarksdale is completely out of keeping with what we've seen of the rest of the town. It's a big house, presumably once a private dwelling and now a B&B, that would be more at home in the Surrey stockbroker belt. It claims to be historic but looks like something built by Wimpey in the 1960s. We couldn't find any information about it online, which suggests that whatever history it can boast is less than remarkable. It does, however, have a large, leafy garden and a sun room, well furnished with reading material, for looking out over it through the rain.

The interior arrangement is a bit strange, for a B&B, though it was probably fine when this was a family home. Our bedroom has a small bathroom, shared with the neighbouring bedroom, with a door on either side. You have to make sure the door to the other side is locked, before using the facilities, and you're invariably interrupted midway through whatever you're doing, by someone trying to get in.

Another oddity is that, having been welcomed by the lady of the house when we first checked in, we've seen no sign of the owners since. Breakfast is already laid out when we come down in the morning and consists of coffee from an urn, packets of bagels with long sell-by dates and something that passes for jam in those irritating and environmentally unfriendly little plastic pots.

The fancier American B&Bs do seem to struggle to get the breakfast bit right, in our experience. Either they go to a lot of trouble preparing weird concoctions, made with asparagus, artichokes, spinach and other ingredients that have no business appearing at an early hour. Or, as here, they provide the bare minimum and leave you to it, while they have a lie-in. The best bet is to head for the nearest diner with plenty of local licence plates in the car park, where you should be able to enjoy fresh coffee and a choice of juices, eggs done the way you like them accompanied by crispy bacon or thick cut slices of ham – or, in Tricia's case, a bowl of granola and yoghurt – all served with a smile.

We do at least have interesting company while enjoying the feast on offer here. Two other couples, both of a similar age to us and both American, are also in residence and, like most of their fellow countrymen and women, they're eager to chat. The first subject of enquiry was, of course, Brexit. One couple thought it quite understandable that we would want to distance ourselves from the cheese-eating surrender monkeys and other foreigners with dubious morals and hygiene habits, while the second pair expressed a more nuanced concern about the possible economic implications and the reduction of our influence in the world.

So it came as no surprise, when the conversation moved on to domestic issues, that the couples revealed themselves to be in opposing camps re the merits, achievements and character of their president. We sat back and let them get on with it, as the debate became increasingly lively. Once we'd finished our bagels, we crept away to start our day's activities. We don't think they noticed our absence.

Today's main event was a visit to Dockery Farms. The southernmost point of this trip and a place that claims, with some justification, to be the real birthplace of the blues. It was a memorable expedition, but not in an entirely good way.

The journey from Clarksdale should have taken about an hour. It ended up going on for nearly three. Most of it through more torrential rain, between endless sodden fields. As we thought we were nearing our destination, more or less on schedule, the satnav, which had been such a loyal companion up to this point, decided to take leave of its senses. It directed us off down a side road for several miles, then onto a dirt track, and then onto an even smaller dirt track along the top of a levee, which ended at an impassable flood. Going back required reversing for about a mile, on a slippery and uneven surface barely wider than the car, with a drop off into deep ditches on either side. Tricia would have got out and walked, had there been any available space to get out onto. As it was, she had to content herself with closing her eyes tight and making small, anguished mewing noises. When we finally returned to something resembling an actual road, and could breathe again, a friendly local lady at a DIY store confidently directed us 15 miles in the wrong direction.

The two upsides to this adventure were that Tricia's tolerance, tested to its limits on an excursion she had no wish to make in the first place, proved equal to the challenge. And when we eventually arrived, the rain had stopped.

Where it all began.

Dockery Farms was a huge cotton plantation, operating in the first half of the 20th century. Will Dockery, the man who founded it, was an unusually enlightened owner, by all accounts. He was fair, at least by prevailing standards, in the way he treated the almost exclusively black sharecroppers who worked the land. And he allowed them to hold musical parties in what little free time they had. Charley Patton, otherwise known as 'The Father of the Blues', spent much of his life here, developing his idiosyncratic style and crowd-pleasing showmanship (Hendrix wasn't the first to play his guitar behind his back), before his growing fame took him further afield to perform and record. Drawn by Charley's presence, many other musicians - including Robert Johnson, Son House and a teenage Howlin' Wolf - came to play at the plantation and learn at the feet of the master during the 20s and 30s. And so the roots started to sprout.

Once a self-contained community with some two thousand residents, its own church, store and gas station - even its own currency! - Dockery is now still and deserted. Most signs of its past are long gone, but the big cotton gin has been restored and several other wooden buildings still stand. As does the unused gas station. Inside the gin, a video presentation gave first-hand accounts of what life there had been like. Hard, by the sound of it, but probably far better than it would have been on some other plantations. The Dockery Farms Foundation, led by luminaries such as Rosanne Cash, Quincy Jones and Herbie Hancock, is working on further restoration and development. Let's just hope that, in a few years' time, it won't be Dockeryland with a Charley's Souvenir Emporium and a King o' The Blues Kitchen.

Thankfully the journey back to Clarksdale took the time expected and we even had a glimpse of sunshine as we strolled around the town, pausing to listen to music coming out of bars and cafes, and to get the obligatory photos at the legendary crossroads.

We probably won't come back in the middle of the night.

For once the word 'legendary' is appropriate. The story goes that Robert Johnson, a wannabe but yet-to-be-much-good bluesman in the early 30s, disappeared from the scene for a while. During his time away, he had a midnight rendezvous with the Devil at a lonely crossroads, and a Faustian pact was arranged: Johnson would be granted the gift of extraordinary musical skills and, in return, would give his soul to the Devil. When next seen, he had indeed become extraordinary and the recordings he made, in what remained of his brief life, are regarded as the zenith of Delta blues. His songs, subject to hundreds of covers by everyone from the Stones and Cream to ZZ Top and Cyndi Lauper, have become staples of the blues rock canon. Had he not met an early demise, of unknown causes but allegedly at the hands of a jealous husband, and become the founder member of the 27 Club (populated by famous musicians who have died at that tragically young age), he would have ended up a wealthy man, rather than a pauper.

Whatever mystique this spot may once have possessed has been dissipated by surrounding it with Abe's Bar-B-Q, Church's Chicken, a shabby gas station and off-licence, and the Crossroads Furniture store. And by placing the commemorative sign, complete with outsized guitars bearing little resemblance to any instrument Johnson would actually have played, in the middle of the busiest intersection in town. A couple of dubious characters who were lurking around, eyeing us up like leopards watching grazing gazelles, didn't enhance the vibe either. If Johnson went to the crossroads and fell down on his knees today, he'd either be hit by a truck, mess up his trousers on discarded fast food wrappers or get mugged.

It should be noted that this is just one of several crossroads in Mississippi, which may or may not have been the setting for his reputed transaction with the Devil. There are also, apparently, at least three graveyards housing his remains. From such uncertainties, myths are created.

Song for the day: Charley Patton – 'High Water Everywhere'.

It had to be a Charley Patton song, in honour of today's pilgrimage, and this is probably his best known one – thanks in large part to Dylan's 'High Water (For Charley Patton)' from the 'Love And Theft' album. But this has a particular resonance, after our uncomfortably close encounter with Mississippi's biblical inundations. "Lord, the water done rushed all over", indeed.

Day 20 - DIFFERENT STATES

Clarksdale MS → Hot Springs AR

We finally spotted the waters of the Mississippi some while before we reached the river itself. They've been having unusual rainfall right across the middle of the country since the start of the year. Rivers further north, in Kansas and beyond, have been flooding for some while. Since they nearly all flow into the Mississippi, the consequences are inevitable. We left the state of the same name as we'd found it – in pouring rain and half expecting to see an ark appear through the murk.

Once across the actual Big Muddy (and it really is big, even without the unwanted extensions), we were into Arkansas, where the first order of business was to make yet another musical pilgrimage - to Marvell, the hometown of the great Levon Helm. We'd been told that his childhood home (yet another little wooden cabin, of course), originally in the splendidly named Turkey Scratch, had been moved to somewhere in Marvell and was in the process of being restored. There was also talk of a bronze memorial bust, though that seemed to be in the early stages of planning and was waiting for funds to be raised, before it could be completed.

If you're not already familiar with him, Levon was a drummer, mandolin player and wonderful singer, who rose to fame as a member of Bob Dylan's backing band in the 60s, and was a fundamental part of that band becoming The Band. One of my few real regrets in life is that we never got to attend one of the Midnight Rambles – the events that Levon hosted during his later years in the barn at his home in Woodstock, where he used to be joined by special guests ranging from Mavis Staples to Elvis Costello. Sadly he passed away in 2012, after a long battle with cancer.

On the way into the town, we found the sign that designated a few miles of the road as Levon Helm Memorial Highway. But once there, no-one we spoke with had ever heard of their most (only?) famous son and looked at us as if we were deranged, when we asked about the cabin. We drove around for a while trying to find it, without success.

At least someone here remembers him.

In fact Marvell failed utterly to live up to its name. Half the dwellings there, even some quite substantial and presumably once desirable ones, were going to wrack and ruin. And the Business District, signed from the highway, made Clarksdale look like Fifth Avenue. None of the places appeared to be in operation, and only the occasional faded sign on a broken window gave any indication that there had ever been a business there at all. Heavens knows where they get the pupils to fill the big high school, which Levon once attended. Or what happens to those pupils after they graduate.

Having no need to linger we whizzed halfway across the state, serenaded by his excellent 'Dirt Farmer' album, to Hot Springs, where we were confident that rather more marvellous sights - and some refreshment - would await us. It was a journey of about 150 miles and turned out to be the longest distance we've driven so far without stopping. Not because we were in a desperate rush to reach Hot Springs, but because there was absolutely nothing to stop for.

Arkansas is the third poorest state in America – only Mississippi and West Virginia have a lower per capita income – and the south-eastern corner that we were going through is one of the most impecunious parts of the state. Once made reasonably prosperous by cotton, that wealth has long since disappeared, along with jobs and a significant percentage of the population. It's also lacking in visual interest, being predominantly low-lying and agricultural. Lots of fields, a fair few trees, an occasional river crossing, then more fields and more trees. It had stopped raining, but it was hard to imagine this land would ever be lovely, even on the best of days. It didn't get a chapter in 'The Most Scenic Drives In America'.

After reaching Hot Springs and driving through several variations on the usual combo of malls, gas stations and fast food outlets, it seemed we were facing further disappointment. But then we suddenly found ourselves in the Historic & Arts District - bizarrely quite unsigned, until you were actually there. This was essentially a single street of two halves. On one side, a succession of boutiques, bars and restaurants, which could have been almost anywhere (other than Clarksdale or Marvell). And on the other, Bathhouse Row - a series of imposing and very elegant buildings where people had once taken the waters that give Hot Springs its name, with a big art deco hotel at one end. Behind them were a wooded hill and the raised Grand Promenade walkway. Looking in that direction, it was a very pretty scene.

Hot Springs advertises itself as 'America's First Resort' and it's been a go-to leisure destination since the 1870s, thanks to the lure of the spas for those in need of their health-reviving properties. It soon added to its natural attractions with a host of casinos, which resulted in the town effectively being run by the mob and their associates, in cahoots with a corrupt police force, for six decades. Al Capone was a regular visitor, staying with his entourage at the big hotel, and even turned a nearby dairy into a distillery during Prohibition. Things were cleaned up after World War II and the casinos were finally shut down in 1967. Gambling has been replaced by a year-round programme of cultural and horse racing events. That, and the careful preservation of its architectural heritage, has maintained the town's popularity.

Our first point of interest, however, was Granny's Kitchen on the commercial side of the street. It was a strange combination of downmarket diner and junk shop, with cheap guitars, old toys and unattractive ornaments on display. It should have been in one of the malls on the outskirts of town, rather than in the heart of the Historic & Arts District.

We only went in for a coffee, but the menu highlighted Peach Cobbler, the classic dessert of the South, which I find impossible to resist. I almost regretted falling for it. Either the feisty middle-aged lady who served us thought I looked in need of nourishment – which I probably do, when compared to the average good ol' boy – or they had a job lot of the stuff that they had to use up. The portion I was given would have fed a family (even an American family) and came with several large scoops of ice cream. It was delicious, but it was proof that you can have too much of a good thing. I would have left it unfinished, but feared our waitress's disapproval. Tricia drank her coffee and looked on in horror.

I needed to walk off some of the tsunami of calories that I'd just been hit by, so we crossed the road and took a stroll along the Grand Promenade, enjoying the views and a welcome return of sunshine and warmth. This eventually led us to a reminder of Hot Springs' other great claim to fame, as the boyhood home of future president Bill Clinton. The association has been celebrated with a plaque holding the flags of the nation and of the state – both of which are wrongly depicted in several respects - and a portrait of the man that is shockingly bad, unless it was the winner of a competition for local elementary schools.

As close as a self-respecting lady would want to get to the ex-Prez.

Hot Springs is the southern gateway to a far more scenic part of Arkansas, where the land rises into the Ozarks, an area of mountains, forests and lakes that extends across four states. As we rolled through this delightful landscape, bathed in soft evening light, it hardly seemed possible that this was the same day that had started with flooded flatlands and a deluge.

Our motel for the night had little to remark on, other than its quiet location surrounded by majestic trees and an outdoor swimming pool that resembled a large bowl of pea soup… we decided not to take a dip. But it did have the first self-service laundry room that we've come across on our travels. After three weeks away, it was urgently needed and we were quick to take advantage. Too quick, in fact. It was only after sorting out our washing, getting the appropriate change from reception, loading up the machine and watching with satisfaction as it began its work, that I realised

I'd left the car's keyless ignition fob (the only one we'd been given, so the only way to get into the car and start it) in a trouser pocket, which was now getting a good soaking. An hour of nervous speculation and calculation ensued, before the machine finished its cycle and we were able to check that the fob was still fit for purpose. The pizzas we dined on tasted especially good after that trauma and the ensuing sense of relief.

Song of the day: Levon Helm 'Wide River To Cross'

Not about the Mississippi of course, but still the right song – on several levels – for today's journey from impoverished Mississippi and Arkansas to the opulence of Hot Springs. Even after the ravages of throat cancer, which almost ended his singing career, Levon still had one of the most distinctive, most moving American voices. Authenticity oozes from every note.

Day 21 - THE HIGHWAY THAT'S THE BEST

Hot Springs AR → Chandler OK

A sun-drenched day started with a gentle meander up Arkansas's leafy Scenic Highway (yes, it is in the book). This bit of the journey was made even more gentle by the need to keep a careful distance behind a slow-moving articulated flatbed truck, piled high with massive tree trunks that looked to be completely unsecured. We were sure they would come tumbling off at some point, especially on the steeper inclines, of which there were many.

We had to say a reluctant farewell to the Scenic Highway (though a thankful farewell to the truck) halfway along its 300-mile length and head west along I-40. We needed to cover some quicker miles, after lingering in the Appalachians and on the Blues Trail in Tennessee and Mississippi, or we would be struggling to hit our fixed dates for The Grand Canyon and Vegas.

The freeway follows the Arkansas River, as it cuts a valley through the woody foothills of the Ozarks, and was actually a quite pleasant drive, as multi-lane roads go. But we were still happy to turn off after an hour or so, onto smaller roads that took us north through the peaceful farmlands of Oklahoma. We bought a quick lunch of coffee and handmade sandwiches from a country store, which we enjoyed on a grassy verge by a field of corn. A rusty oil derrick stood in the middle of the field, methodically nodding like a giant metal chicken pecking at grain. We didn't see another soul or another vehicle while we were there, apart from a battered old truck with a piece of unidentifiable machinery on the back, which gave us a cheery toot of the horn as it passed.

If this wasn't enough to tell us that we were in the very heart of the heartland, we soon saw signs for Muskogee, a medium-size town (sorry, city) immortalised in Merle Haggard's 'Okie From Muskogee'. Merle was disingenuous about his motivation for writing the song, but whatever his intentions it has become an archetypal redneck anthem – "We don't burn no draft cards down on Main Street, we like livin' right and bein' free". So

Muskogee has become known the world over, even though hardly anyone could tell you where it is or anything about it.

Our target for the day was Route 66, the thoroughfare without which no American road trip would be truly complete. Sadly (and surprisingly, given Americans' efforts to respect and even embellish their limited history in other respects) little of its original two and a half thousand miles between Chicago and Los Angeles remains intact. Long stretches have disappeared under freeways and what's left has few reminders of its iconic role as The Mother Road, taking folk fleeing the Depression and Dust Bowl of the 1930s to a new life in California or by the Great Lakes, or as a place to get your kicks in the fun-loving, free-spirited 50s.

Apparently the owner inspired a character in Pixar's 'Cars'.

One of the best preserved bits according to 'Road Trip USA', a magisterial tome that's been another guiding light on this adventure, lies in the 80-odd miles between Tulsa and Oklahoma City. We joined it at a busy junction in Sapulpa, a few miles outside Tulsa, where only a small sign on a wall at one corner let us know we turning on to Route 66, and a much bigger one told us we were at 'The Crossroads of America'. Apparently this was because the last bit of road we'd come in on was, unbeknown to us, Highway 75. In the pre-freeway era this had been the main north/south highway, from the Canada right down to the Gulf, and its intersection with its east/west equivalent would indeed have been a landmark.

Route 66 soon took us out into the Oklahoma countryside again and we had it almost to ourselves, as the great majority of traffic is now carried by the I-44 turnpike that runs more or less parallel with it, keeping a discreet distance. The road ambles between lush pastures that are a far cry from the desolate scenes of the 1930s or the action-packed thoroughfare of the '50s. The one constant reminder of those times are the road markers. They feature a map of this oddly contoured state, shaped like a hand with its index finger pointing the way west.

Echoes of the past can still be seen in the little towns along the way, however, such as the Rock Cafe in Stroud, built using stones from the original highway; the Boom-a-rang Diner in Chandler, where we'll have breakfast tomorrow; the restored Phillips 66 gas station across the street; and the Lincoln Motel, which is where we're spending the night.

We stopped for photos at the Rock Café and were slightly disappointed to find that most sight lines were impeded by crudely executed 2D cartoon cars, placed right in front of the building. It seems the café, or at least its owner, had inspired the makers of the Pixar movie 'Cars', and they've been dining out – or rather, dining in – on it ever since. We felt obliged to go with the flow and take some silly shots, pretending to sit inside the vehicles.

The Lincoln, when we got there, had done a more faithful job of keeping its character, for better and for worse. It's a piece of living, working memorabilia, in continuous operation since the 30s. The row of neat yellow chalets, each with a wrought iron bench outside, looked much as it must have done when first built, and the handsome neon sign at the front was a direct throwback to the classic style of the '50s. The rooms inside the chalets weren't the biggest and the bathroom also seemed as if it hadn't seen much change over the decades. But the price we'd paid felt closer to 1939 than 2019, so it would have been churlish to complain.

Stepping into a past where wi-fi was unknown.

Authenticity was taken a bit too far, though, when it came to a complete lack of functioning wi-fi in our room, despite the promise on the noticeboard by the entrance. The Indian chap who checked us in spent some considerable time trying to resolve the issue, without success. I ended up having to perch on the steps of his office with my laptop balanced on my knees, to get just enough signal to research our accommodation options for tomorrow and somewhere to eat tonight. (Should we envy all those travellers who stayed here back in the day, without dreaming of such problems? Or should we pity their primitive, unconnected lives? I'd usually favour simplicity and innocence, but there never seems to be progress without some loss.)

When I say 'Indian chap', by the way, I mean Asian Indian not Native American. It would have been interesting to found out how he ended up here, about as far as it's possible to get from any of the usual entry points into the States, and how he was assimilating into the local culture. Judging by his accent, he hadn't been in Chandler long. But he was getting increasingly flustered by the wi-fi's lack of co-operation and I didn't want to take up any more of his day. We also needed to get some photos sharpish, before a looming storm reached us and the dramatic light disappeared.

The rain soon forced us back inside where, with no web browsing to keep us occupied and only more bad news about the weather or more one-eyed ranting about (and from) the president on TV, we had to make our own amusement. Tricia played a game on her iPad, which seemed to be causing quite a lot of agitation and anxiety, while I immersed myself in the scenic drives that we have to look forward to – we're exactly halfway through the trip now, but it seems like we've still got a long way to go and a whole lot of good stuff in store.

Song for the day: Vince Gill – 'The Old Lucky Diamond Motel'

In an effort to avoid the bleedin' obvious, here's a song about the loss of a Route 66 landmark. Gill is coy about whether or not it's a true story, but he's an Oklahoma boy and a part-time member of The Time Jumpers (see Day 14), though sadly not on the night we saw them. So this will do nicely.

Day 22 - GOING WEST

Chandler OK → McLean TX

Today was a Route 66 day from start to finish. To be honest, a fair bit of it was spent eating up the miles, going west along I-40 from Oklahoma City towards Amarillo. But that runs over the bones of what was once the old road, so we reckon it should count.

At least we kicked off and ended with the real deal. We woke up in one of the last remaining original motels (est. 1939) and went to bed in another (est. 1956); we had breakfast in a proper old school diner; and our evening meal was eaten at a rustic steakhouse in a tiny Texas town.

The Boom-a-rang Diner, a stone's throw from our motel, was a straight shot back to the '50s, from the red Naugahyde seating to the retro signage. The service, though amiable, was a bit slow. Not that it mattered. We were quite happy to drink our coffee and take in the photos and posters decorating the walls. These mostly revolved around the superstars of the age: Marilyn, Marlon, Elvis… the usual suspects. You know you've achieved iconic status when your first name is enough to identify you.

The breakfasts, when they arrived – a stack of pancakes with maple syrup for Tricia, 'Elvin's Ultimate' (a pig-out of multiple eggs, bacon, sausages, hash browns, toast and biscuits) for me – were more than enough to set us up for the day. The portions only get bigger, the further you get from either coast.

A sign by the door, as we waddled out, read 'You are about to return to the harsh realities of the real world'. Even if this was melodramatic we were sad to think, not for the first time on this trip, that we would probably never pass this way again.

Over the next few hours we also called in on three recommended sources of information - the Route 66 Interpretive Center in Chandler, the impressively restored Round Barn in Arcadia and the National Route 66 Museum in Elk City. In that order.

The Interpretive Center was housed in what used to be the Chandler Armoury. The guy who greeted us gave a lecture on the history of the building, which threatened to go on forever, until we were mercifully spared by the arrival of another couple. When we managed to get inside, the highlight was a record, in words, photos and home movies, of one man's post-grad road trip in the '50s. It was richly evocative of Route 66 in its heyday, all the more so as we were able to watch it in comfort, lounging on old car seats.

Getting our kicks on Route 66.

The Round Barn had pretty much fallen apart, judging by the photos on display, before being restored during the '90s. The folk who put it back together won a National Preservation Honor Award for the work and boy, did they deserve it. The stunning interior of the domed roof, made up of countless strips of wood and looking a bit like an upturned wicker basket, was alone worth the price of admission. (Actually, admission was free – we just made a donation to the restoration/maintenance fund.) Apparently it's now the most photographed landmark anywhere on Route 66.

The Elk City museum was the only one of the three 'attractions' to sell tickets. In fairness it was by far the biggest, with displays of everything from old cars to reconstructed dwellings. We were the only visitors, at the back end of a Wednesday afternoon, however, and the ladies running the place made us feel we were stopping them from shutting up and getting on with the rest of their day. In fact they did start closing sections of the museum, before we completed our tour and before the advertised time.

Each of these places had a wealth of memorabilia - signage, artefacts, film clips and pics of old shops, restaurants, motels, gas stations, etc - and did a fine job of bigging up their particular town's place in Route 66 history. But there was no mention anywhere of the road's central role in the cataclysmic events of the '30s, as immortalised by John Steinbeck and Woody Guthrie. We were hoping to see some of Dorothea Lange's photographs and other records. There's a wealth of extraordinary shots from that period – just go the Images section of bing.com and put in 'dust bowl'. But, other than one exhibit in Elk City, which actually highlighted the 'Grapes Of Wrath' movie... not a thing.

We wondered if this was further evidence that America is in lockstep with its president and can't bear losers. The poor souls who were California bound - not only from Oklahoma, but also from Kansas, Texas and elsewhere - with what they could save of their belongings after the dust storms, were certainly that. It's estimated that 3.5 million people moved away from the Great Plains in the aftermath of the Dust Bowl, most of them following this road.

Our afternoon drive took us through the area worst affected by those storms. In the west of Oklahoma and into Texas, the terrain becomes completely flat. Grasslands stretched to distant horizons in every direction, under an infinite bowl of fierce blue sky. Trees were few and far between. It's now prosperous cattle country. Back then it was being intensively cultivated, mainly for wheat, with disastrous consequences. The grasses that had always held the soil together were stripped out; long periods of drought ruined the crops and turned the soil to dust; and the winds carried that dust right across the country in great clouds. It reached as far as New York and, around here, buried vehicles completely and houses up to the roof.

A happier step back in time awaited us when we got to McLean, our first stop in Texas. The town has always been small and got even smaller, after the freeway bypassed it in the '80s. The population is now less than 800 and shrinking. So we had no trouble finding The Cactus Inn, the only accommodation in town, especially as it had a 20ft effigy of a cactus erected outside it. Once there, however, we weren't quite sure what, if anything, to expect. When I'd called to book a room 24 hours earlier, I'd just got an answerphone, and their minimalist website didn't have online booking. But the photos we'd seen made it look just like we'd want a genuine Route 66 motel to be, so we were determined to give it a go.

The unmissable Cactus Tree Motel

There were no other vehicles anywhere around when we arrived and, even less auspiciously, the door to reception was locked. All it needed was tumbleweed blowing through the parking lot. We were beginning to wonder how far it would be to the next hotel, when the door opened and an old lady tottered out, followed by a girl of about 10, who bounded across to greet us. She was full of questions, which only intensified when she realised we weren't just strangers to these parts but not even American.

Her effusiveness and the old lady's unfamiliarity with the checking-in process – "Now where'd ah put those dang keys?", "Sorry, suh, I don't thank we kin take tham thar credit cards, jest cayush" – made us suspect that the Cactus Inn doesn't get too many visitors. It should. The room was a decent size and well kept. The bathroom was reasonably modern and clean. The wi-fi was stable and fast. And the amount of 'cayush' we handed over was less than $50.

To complete our satisfaction The Red River Steakhouse, right next door, was terrific. We seemed to be the only people there who hadn't come in wearing big hats. And fortunately, as we hadn't eaten since our whopping breakfasts, we were able to do justice to the plate-filling steaks.

Song for the day: Bruce Springsteen – 'The Ghost Of Tom Joad'

Something by Woody Guthrie might have been the first choice, for a day spent tracing the footsteps and tyre tracks of the 30s migration. But, since that history seems to have been allowed to vanish into the ether, a song about the ghosts of the people who participated in it feels like the right call.

Day 23 - I CAN SEE FOR MILES

McLean TX → Clayton NM

There wasn't much to write home about on the 250 miles from McLean TX to Clayton NM. One mile of flat, featureless farm country looks much the same as another.

A sight which certainly did interrupt the tedium was Cadillac Ranch, perhaps the most celebrated art installation in the world, sitting right alongside I-40/Route 66, just outside Amarillo. First created in 1974, with sponsorship from a local millionaire, it's a row of ten Cadillacs, dating from the late 40s to the early 60s, half buried in the ground with their tail fins sticking out. It used to be in the middle of a corn field, but was moved to its current site in 1997, as the growth of the city threatened to engulf it.

They won't open up their engines and let 'em roar again.

The original look of the cars has been changed many times over the years. Sometimes being repainted for filming or to mark a particular occasion, and sometimes being restored to something resembling their original condition. We regret to report that they're currently covered with graffiti, which visitors are encouraged to embellish. A jerry-built stall at the entrance was selling cans of spray paint, as well as postcards and other mass-produced souvenirs. As a result, the whole area is littered with discarded cans and, as another onlooker remarked, smells like a toxic waste dump. With the cars also surrounded by large puddles, after all the recent rain, it's not what you'd call a pretty sight, but it's still a photo op not to be missed. Whether The Boss would have been inspired to write a song about it now, though, is open to question.

The only other thing that particularly caught our attention was a freight train, running on a track that was parallel to the road, after we left Amarillo. To say it was long would be the wildest of understatements. Its two ends would probably have spanned the borders of some English counties. Even though we were going in opposite directions, at 50mph, it took a good five minutes to pass each other by completely.

On relatively uneventful days like today, we had hoped to get a flavour of the real America by listening to the radio as we drove. In my head I was hearing Wolfman Jack and Murray the K, stations specialising in everything from country to jazz, and playlists that weren't dictated by research. In reality, all we could find was classic rock (think Bon Jovi and Eagles, rather than Buddy and Elvis); country of the 'new' poppy, formulaic kind; and men (always men) bellowing about faith, while exhorting their listeners to demonstrate that faith by donating generously. Each option on the dial came with regular interruptions for ads selling legal assistance and miracle cures for embarrassing ailments, followed by detailed terms, conditions and caveats, delivered at a frenetic gabble that made them unintelligible. Maybe that is a flavour of America in the here and now, but it's not to our taste.

Thankfully we'd brought a stash of CDs with us and our car had a reasonably good sound system. We hadn't felt much need for them, thus far, but now their moment had come. The albums are evenly divided between Tricia's choices and mine. We alternated between them as we ate up the miles.

Her selections, predictably, consist exclusively of Beatles, Beatles spin-offs (Wings, Travelling Wilburys), Beatles soundalikes (ELO) and runners-up in the 'Best Pop Bands of the 60s' stakes (Beach Boys, Bee Gees). Mine, with a far bigger library to select from (at least it extends beyond the letter B!), concentrated on albums that should be relevant to our pilgrimages, while considerately avoiding stuff that would have Tricia reaching for the 'eject' button. So Dolly, Johnny and the countryfied Grateful Dead are travelling with us. Captain Beefheart, Tom Waits and God Bless You Black Emperor are not.

Another way of passing the journey lay in speculating on what life might be like, in the isolated ranch houses and small towns we were seeing. Channing TX was a classic example, apparently consisting of nothing more than a gas station with a store attached, a towering white grain elevator and some huge metal cylinders, which may have been storage for the grain or for silage – we didn't want to think about it too much. We were ready for something to drink so, with no other alternatives in sight and many miles to go before the next community, we stopped and went into the store.

Two kids in their late teens or early 20s, one boy and one girl, were staffing the checkout. Their impassive, dead-eyed gaze followed us as we chose our purchases and didn't change for an instant when we went to pay. I don't believe they uttered a word in the whole time we were there, to each other or to us, other than to tell us the total cost of our items. We wondered whether they might be the offspring of Cleetus the Slack-Jawed Yokel, from The Simpsons. They were surely too young to have lost the will to live. But when we stepped outside again, into the desolate surroundings and broiling heat, we could understand it. Being born here probably wouldn't be a winning ticket in the lottery of life.

One clue as to how people survive in these unpromising conditions, without succumbing to depression or insanity, lay in the number of churches and other places of worship. As the radio had shown us, religion is both a top priority and big business in the so-called Bible Belt of the South. Well over 80% of Texans say that religion is important to them. Even if some of them are doing that for the sake of appearances, the fact that they feel the need to say it tells you something. Ask the same question in the UK and you'd be lucky to get 8% answering in the positive. And the remainder would have no shame at all about their negative response.

Another indication of reasons to be cheerful was the high school football stadium in Dalhart, the last town of any size in Texas before we crossed into New Mexico. Dalhart has a population of 8000, which the stadium could have accommodated with plenty of room to spare. Any English football team below Championship level, with the possible exception of Sunderland, would be delighted to have such a home... and the passionate following, from miles around, that no doubt goes with it. It put me in mind of 'Friday Night Lights', one of the best TV series I've ever watched, about a Texas backwater much like this one and its high school football team. That show made existence in a town like this, with its community spirit and easy affluence, seem quite pleasant. We could only hope, for the sake of Dalhart's residents, that it was an accurate reflection.

By the time we reached Clayton, the sight of snow-capped mountains in the distance offered the promise of better things to come tomorrow, as we start the New Mexico North scenic drive. And Clayton itself was an unexpectedly pleasant place to spend the night.

It was once an important point on the Santa Fe Trail, a major trade route between east and west in the mid-19th century, so had a colourful history, which we learned about during an early evening stroll round the town. The most notable – and without doubt the most grotesque – tale concerned the execution of 'Black Jack' Ketchum in 1901.

Black Jack was one of the last legendary outlaws of the Old West, with a particular penchant for robbing trains. When he was finally caught and sentenced to hang, it was Clayton's first hosting of such an event. Tickets were sold, as well as souvenir dolls. The executioners' inexperience showed, however. They forgot to remove the heavy sandbag that they'd used for practice, so the combined weight of bag and the condemned man's body caused a drop of such ferocity that Black Jack was decapitated. He was the last man in America to hang for train robbery and the only one to lose his head to the gallows.

Black Jack's head, thankfully, not on display.

He also featured prominently at the Hotel Eklund, another main player in Clayton's history, where we went for dinner. The establishment had kept its character, with plenty of old wood panelling and period furnishings, the remains of once magnificent beasts on the walls and a long bar, perfect for sliding whisky glasses along. And they fed us well.

Song for the day: John Mellencamp – 'Small Town'

Mellencamp is one of the bards of Middle America, and this song sums up both the positives and negatives of life in the countless small towns scattered across the heartland, such as the ones we've passed through today. Lou Reed and John Cale did a different song, with the same title, as part of their tribute album to Andy Warhol. But Lou's acerbic New York cynicism has no place out here.

Day 24 - COMING LIKE A GHOST TOWN

Clayton NM → Taos NM

After two days of travelling across the seemingly endless grasslands of Oklahoma and Texas, it was a joy to see the Sangre de Cristo mountains rising ahead of us. One of the things we love most about living in the UK is that the landscape never stays the same for long, wherever you go. The same can't be said for much of the United States, so the prospect of some variety was eagerly anticipated.

Sangre de Cristo is Spanish for 'blood of Christ' – the Spanish were the first Europeans to explore and settle the western side of the continent. It's thought that the name comes from the colour that the peaks can take on, at sunrise and sunset, especially when they're covered with snow. Or it could relate to the colour of oak leaves in autumn, on the trees covering the slopes at lower levels. As we were seeing the mountains in full daylight and late spring, we didn't observe either of these possibilities. They were beautiful, though.

The road through Cimarron Canyon was described by our 'Most Scenic Drives In America' guide as being the prettiest stretch of the New Mexico North route. However, a massive fire had burned through tens of thousands of acres last summer, forcing the temporary evacuation of the town of Cimarron. If we'd been doing this journey then, as first intended, the canyon would have been impassable and we'd have been looking at a significant detour.

The aftermath of the fire was all too evident. Scorched, skeletal trunks in their thousands lined the road. But Mother Nature's amazing recuperative powers could also be seen. From eye level upwards, everything was in shades of grey and black, apart from the deep blue sky. Yet at ground level new life was springing back from the ashes, in a full array of colours. Give it another couple of years and you'll probably never know the fire had happened.

Eagle Nest, the next place after the canyon and mercifully untouched by the blaze, was far more like it. Lying between the mountains and a glistening lake, it boasted what looked like an enticing run of cafes, bars and shops along the main street. A pitstop was clearly required.

Despite the name, Eagle Nest was not the high point of our trip.

As soon as we got out of the car, we knew we'd misjudged our attire for the day. Without realising it, we'd climbed to above 8000 feet and the temperature had dropped sharply, even with the sun at its height. Shorts and sleeveless tops were no longer adequate. I was willing to tough it out, but Tricia, being less well insulated and notoriously intolerant of cold, was in urgent need of a costume change. We asked a lady, standing at her garden gate chatting to a neighbour, where we might find a rest room for this purpose and were directed down a side street to the Senior Center.

While Tricia went to put on extra layers of clothing, I wandered round the building. Although it had seemed empty when we first arrived, this was not the case. The main hall was thronged with elderly people sitting at communal tables. The lack of noise was due to the fact that they were all focused on tucking into a free meal, provided for oldies in reduced circumstances. One of the helpers greeted me cheerily and wanted to know if I'd come for mine. The encounter suggested two things: that Eagle Nest might not be the idyllic, comfortable community it appeared to be; and that I'm kidding myself in thinking I look younger than my years.

Once Tricia was protected against the elements, we said goodbye to my new friend and went in search of refreshment. Maybe even a little retail therapy. And it soon became clear that the town did indeed have issues. Almost every single establishment on the main street, which had looked so enticing at first glance, was closed and/or for sale. Just as we were about to give up hope, we found a little diner at the very end of the strip, which was still active and serving good coffee. Unsurprisingly it was popular with those locals who weren't eating for free at the Senior Center. Again, none of them looked to be under seventy. As we drank our coffee, all the talk at other tables was of the town's demise and plans for getting out.

A couple of miles outside Eagle Nest was Elizabethtown – an actual ghost town, rather than one in waiting – formerly a community of over 7000, drawn first by copper mining and then by the gold in tham thar hills, complete with a school, churches, stores, what must have been quite a grand hotel and, of course, a choice of saloons. It gradually shrank, as the ore ran out, and was abandoned by the late '30s. Only a few buildings remain and the population now seemed to consist of a small group of folk from a nearby ranch, who were trying to renovate the place as a potential attraction and were happy to give us an account of its history.

A prime property in Elizabethtown – we resisted the urge to buy.

A little further on, as the valley broadened out, our attention was caught by a large white structure, on a rise next to the road. We followed the side turning that led up to it and found ourselves at the Vietnam Veterans Memorial. Not the famous one in Washington DC, obviously, but one that pre-dates it by a good ten years. The white building we'd seen from below was a chapel and beneath it, lying underground, was an exhibition space with information about the Vietnam War and the history of the Memorial.

From this, and from chatting with other visitors, we found out that it was the work of a couple who had owned a nearby ranch. Their son, 1st Lt David Westphall, had been killed in action in 1968, and they'd decided to use his life insurance money to create this lasting memorial to him and his comrades. Apparently they had to overcome a lot to get it completed – both financial obstacles and general antipathy, at a time when the Vietnam War was deeply unpopular and celebrating any aspect of it was not the done thing.

It's now a fine spot for remembrance and contemplation, with sweeping views along the valley and across to the surrounding mountains. Especially touching is the Veterans Memorial Walkway in the well-kept gardens, lined with many bricks carrying the names of those who served and died during America's various wars. David's parents would surely be looking down with satisfaction at how their tribute to their son has been carried on. If we'd been here in a few days' time, on Memorial Day, we'd have been joined by about 20,000 bikers paying their annual respects as part of an organised rally.

Our final destination for the day was Taos, a renowned hub of arts and crafts, which is anything but deserted. Ansell Adams, Georgia O'Keeffe, D.H. Lawrence and Carl Jung are just a few of the illustrious names, who have lived and worked here. More recently it's become a tourist mecca, with more chic hotels, fancy restaurants, pricey galleries and bijou boutiques than you can shake a stick at. The resident population is around 6000, but at any given time there are probably at least twice that number of people in the town.

It seems strange that Eagle Nest, which has an even more scenic location plus a lake and a better name, should be dying on its arse while Taos thrives. Why have all those artists and all those tourists come here, rather than there? Perhaps we'll get some explanation tomorrow, when we explore the latter in greater depth.

Song for the day: Waylon Jennings – 'Taos, New Mexico'

We can't go all the way without a song from one of American music's legendary exponents. Waylon was born in Texas, died in Arizona and – like most country artists – found fame in Nashville. But it seems he came to Taos, unless this is complete fiction, and had a memorable visit. As, hopefully, will we.

Day 25 - A JOURNEY THROUGH THE PAST

Taos NM

After enjoying the breakfast at Casa Benavides, our hotel, which seems to have a big reputation in Taos, we headed out to sample the wealth of galleries and boutiques. We won't bore you with the details, save to say that silver & turquoise jewellery, objects d'art with Native American motifs and bad paintings in garish colours were much in evidence. One shop's offering was much the same as the next's. On the positive side, most of the stuff was produced somewhere in the United States, rather than in China.

An opportunity to sit down beats another opportunity for retail therapy.

A particular favourite, represented across many media, was a silhouetted figure with what might have been a feathered headdress and an unfeasibly large nose. This, we were told, was Kokopelli, a Native American deity associated with fertility in all its senses, from conceiving children to raising crops. In much earlier representations, found on cave walls and artefacts from archaeological digs, he also had a monstrous phallus, as often seems to be the case with pre-historic figures of cultural significance. In the modern, commercialised version, the genitalia have gone and the big nose has been re-interpreted as a flute that Kokopelli is playing. We don't want any more children and we're not planning on becoming farmers, so we didn't feel the need for his divine assistance, via a t-shirt or a mug or any other form of souvenir.

The only offering that really stood out, and which we'd have loved to buy, would have been impossible to get home. This was a range of solid copper lampshades, handmade by a New Mexico company. None of them would have fitted into a suitcase and, when we asked about having one shipped to the UK, the cost – when added to the not inconsiderable price of a shade – was prohibitive. I emailed the makers a bit later, while we had a coffee, to see if they have distribution in the UK. Sadly, they don't.

Ambling round the town was an agreeable way to spend the morning, though, even if the retail therapy became repetitive. All the earth-coloured adobe buildings, old and new, gave the town a pleasing uniformity of look, reminiscent of Cotswold villages and their consistent use of golden stone. And, as with those villages, Taos took on a gorgeous lustre in the sunshine.

Then on to what may well be the main reason for the success of this particular spot in attracting artists, writers and, more recently, tourists.

The Taos Pueblo, a couple of miles out of town, is the only place anywhere in the States to have both National Historic Landmark and UNESCO World Heritage Site status. Most of it is at least 500 years old and some of it nearly a thousand. That's historic by anyone's standards.

The village is quite extensive, sitting on both sides of Red Willow Creek - usually a small stream but currently a whirling torrent, with sandbags standing by, after all the rain that's been sweeping across the States. The condition of the buildings, some of them multi-storey blocks, speaks volumes for the quality and durability of adobe architecture.

A few of the houses are still lived in, although not full time. According to tradition, no electricity or running water are allowed inside the Pueblo, so the people with homes here also have somewhere outside the village, with 21st century facilities.

A lot of the other former dwellings are used as shops. These ranged from a man with one arm squatting on his porch, offering a handful of small clay bears, to a multi-roomed emporium selling much the same selection of arts and crafts as the stores in town. It was noticeable that, in comparison to similar outlets in most other countries, not one of the owners made any attempt to recommend their wares to us. This was actually very refreshing, but you couldn't help thinking that this laidback approach was inhibiting the success of their businesses. For their own sakes they should probably get one of the carpet vendors, who we met in Morocco, to give them a master class in high pressure sales techniques, delivered with an ingratiating smile.

In ancient footsteps at Taos Pueblo

The most enjoyable part of the visit - other than simply taking in the views of this ancient place, with its even more ancient mountain backdrop - was a long conversation with a lady running one of the shops. She told us about the tribe's efforts to maintain its culture and of a happyish ending to their part in the more typically tragic Native American saga.

They had, of course, been robbed of their land over the years, by a combination of force and legal decree. President Teddy Roosevelt's government took a huge chunk of it in 1906, to become part of the National Forest network. But, starting in the '70s, they've managed to make the law work for them in getting some of it back. Nearly 100,000 acres are now under their control, including the sacred Blue Lake, which is a central part of their belief system. The War Chief wing of the Tribal

Council is entrusted with protecting their borders from any new encroachment. By peaceful means, despite their name.

We got back to Casa Benavides in time for tea and cakes, and found ourselves sitting next to a couple from New Jersey. He looked and sounded like an archetypal New York cabbie – an archetypal New York cabbie who isn't Puerto Rican or claiming to be Eastern European royalty, that is. Which was misleading, as they were both retired schoolteachers. Another Brexit-to-Trump conversation ensued, which revolved mainly around his thesis that neither Boris nor Donald expected to win their respective votes and had only embarked on their campaigns in the interests of self-promotion. We weren't about to disagree. Though we had to remind ourselves that one of the benefits of being away from home at the moment is the absence of round-the-clock coverage of the Brexit fiasco, and make a mental note to keep such conversations to a minimum, whenever possible.

After eating last night in a suave, upmarket place, overlooking the Plaza in the centre of town, we decided to go for something more down-to-earth this evening. We went to a well-reviewed place, tucked away down a side alley, which promised live music as well as authentic regional cuisine. When we got there it was a pretty funky place, with a lively atmosphere that boded well.

Tricia, never the most adventurous of diners, turned her nose up at the authentic side of the menu and chose a burger. Which, in fairness, looked pretty good and reportedly was. I, on the other hand, felt obliged to get down with the vibe and went for enchiladas. In theory I should be a big fan of Mexican food. I like spicy and I like a variety of ingredients and textures on my plate. The problem is that, whatever you order, it seems to be the same thing – tortillas with your choice of filling and sides of refried beans and rice – and, most damagingly, it looks like someone has already eaten and evacuated it. I know all those food shows on TV bang on about how flavour is the main thing, but aesthetics surely come into it too and, in terms of presentation, the Mexicans probably take the wooden spoon in the hotly contested global cuisine challenge. What I had did taste OK, but I was glad we were eating in one of the murkier corners of a dimly lit room.

Midway through our meal, the evening's entertainment arrived and started setting up on the small bandstand next to the bar. We'd been hoping for something with a local twist, or at least something acoustic and rootsy. The superfluity of tattoos and piercings, sported by the young men assembling a quantity of amplification that was quite out of keeping with the size of the venue, suggested this was not what we would be getting. And it wasn't. I'm not completely averse to music driven by anger, even when incoherently expressed, and I'm a veteran of several Motorhead gigs, so volume holds few fears. This was neither the time nor the place for such shenanigans, however. We gave the band the benefit of the doubt through their first number and, when the start of the second one was indistinguishable from it, we left. Tricia, who doesn't favour shouty, melody-free stuff in the slightest, couldn't get out fast enough. We could still hear them roaring and ranting, halfway back to our hotel.

Song for the day: Woody Guthrie – 'This Land Is Your Land'

We had to have this one, at some point of the journey and, after getting up close and personal with descendants of this land's original, dispossessed inhabitants, today feels like the right moment. Considered by many to be America's alternative national anthem, it's the song that's made Woody immortal.

Day 26 - LAND OF A THOUSAND VISTAS

Taos NM → Farmington NM

Today's drive of 200 miles, from Taos to Farmington, took us through an exhilarating array of New Mexico landscapes, as the latest of our Most Scenic Drives lived up to its billing.

The journey began with the sagebrush strewn Taos Plateau. When you first come to it, this appears to be ten miles of complete, uninterrupted flatness, with mountains at either side. Then, without warning, you realise that the plateau is split in half by the Rio Grande Gorge. A 600ft deep gash in the land, it's now spanned by the Rio Grande Gorge Bridge, which vibrates alarmingly when trucks go over it. But one can only imagine how dispiriting it must have been for the early settlers, to have struggled through the Sangre de Cristo mountains and reached what looked like a nice, easy stretch of travel, only to have this impassable obstacle suddenly appear in front of them.

Although you can hike in and out of the Gorge, on trails which have probably been there for centuries, you wouldn't want to do it with wagons and cattle and families. So they would have had to go either north or south through the mountains on a long detour, before they found themselves in a valley with an easier crossing.

Whatever those settlers might have felt when they got to the Gorge, however, it can't have been as bad as what some more recent arrivals have been experiencing. The bridge has become a suicide hotspot, averaging a minimum of two deaths a year. Various ways of reducing this tragic statistic have been proposed, from high fencing along either side of the bridge to netting beneath it, but when we were there the only preventative measures in place were crisis hotline call boxes and 'Hazardous Area' signs (just as well they warned us, we'd never have guessed!), announcing that the state of New Mexico takes no responsibility for any injuries or losses suffered. The barriers running along the bridge were barely more than waist high. You could imagine someone toppling over by accident, as they lean backwards to take a selfie. Deliberately scaling them would be easy. The Taos Search & Rescue team had recovered another body from the river below, only three weeks earlier.

Putting aside such grim thoughts, the Gorge was a fantastically photogenic landmark, and we spent some while going over and around it, in search of the best shots.

Trying not to look down from the Rio Grande Gorge Bridge.

The terrain rose again, as we left the plateau, and we passed through immaculately manicured meadows, fringed with the pine and aspen of the Carson National Forest, where cattle grazed and drank from a meandering creek. Then up and over the Brazos Summit, a pass between the mountain peaks at 10,000 ft, with snow still thick on the ground. It looked beautiful, but getting out of the car for photos was a near freezing slap in the face. We were grateful that we'd dressed more appropriately for altitude today.

As the road dropped down from the summit, we came to the Brazos Cliffs, two thousand feet of sheer rock formed by volcanic eruptions many millions of years ago. Apparently they're popular with the climbing fraternity. I've never felt less urge to join them. The signs at the beginning and end of the National Forest hailed it as 'Land of Many Uses', which seemed both too vague and too prosaic for a place of such majestic splendour.

Once we'd reached lower levels we were ready for a warming cup of coffee. The only town for miles, however, was Dulce. At first sight this looked to be yet another community consisting of a gas station, an auto repair shop, a church and little else. Then, just off the main road, we spotted a big casino. Then a bigger community centre. Then an even bigger administration building. And then an even bigger supermarket, which turned out to have a cafe inside. All of them quite new.

We'd arrived in the heart of the Jicarilla Apache Nation. The tribe once inhabited a huge area, across what are now the states of Colorado, New Mexico, Texas, Oklahoma and Kansas, leading a mostly peaceful, semi-nomadic existence. By the late 1800s, they'd lost the lot and had to beg the government for a reservation. Surprise, surprise, what they were given was not fit for anything that would adequately support human life, and the tribe was almost starved into extinction. Then came the discovery of oil and gas on the reservation. That, along with compensation for the loss of their land won through the courts, has allowed them to make a recovery. The development we saw in Dulce clearly demonstrates that the Jicarillas must now be getting a fair amount of money from somewhere, whether that be the casino, natural resources or the government. Either way, they made good coffee at the café and the only palefaces in the town were made to feel a lot more welcome than our ancestors, who first wrested this land from the natives.

The town is particularly known for the so-called Dulce Base. According to conspiracy theorists, this is a huge, top secret installation under the mountains overlooking the town, controlled by malevolent alien forces. Various extravagant rumours about the base are in circulation, relating to such far-fetched notions as the presence of human-alien and human-animal hybrids, horrific genetic experimentation, firefights between the aliens and US military, and a subway network that links this base to others all over the country. Photos, video footage and first or second-hand reports claiming to support these yarns circulate from time to time. The Dulce authorities do nothing to dispel the rumours, as the search for the base and its supposed occupants is yet another draw for tourists.

We saw no sign of seven feet tall, man-eating grey creatures from another planet as we left Dulce, though one of the guys in the supermarket was lanky and looked a bit peaky. Just the wooded hills, rocky outcrops and dry arroyos of the tribal territory, reminiscent of the settings for the old TV westerns ('Lone Ranger', 'Range Rider' and the like) that I loved as a boy. Then the road led out into a much wider valley, bordered by high sandstone cliffs, and took us to Farmington, our home for the night. All in all, a proper scenic drive.

'Land of Natural Splendours' might be a better tag line.

It's days like this that make us realise how blessed we are, to live in an age of affordable and convenient international travel, and a time of relative peace in which to pursue it. My parents were great lovers of nature and beauty in all its forms. They would have revelled in some of the places we're seeing on this journey, but they never got beyond the bits of Western Europe that are most accessible from the UK. Even those excursions were only very occasional and, in my Dad's case, under less than ideal circumstances for the most part, during and after World War II.

Tricia's father actually got all the way to America at more or less the same time, to do training for service with the RAF. He was much less of an outdoors man, however, and his wartime experience seems to have revolved primarily around the jazz clubs of New York, where he was privileged to see several of the greats in action – Duke Ellington, Count

Basie, etc. We'd felt closer to him while we were on our tour of Greenwich Village.

More blessings were in store when we arrived at our B&B, which was further evidence that what you pay for accommodation is no guarantee of what you're going to get.

The Casa Blanca Inn was barely half the price of Casa Benavides in Taos, and a fraction of what we'd forked out in New York, yet it was way better. Our room was spacious and comfortable, with a big sunken bath. The communal area had a choice of refreshments available 24/7. There was a lovely patio, centred on a fountain, which caught the last of the sun as we arrived and was the perfect spot for a much-needed cold beer. And we got an excellent suggestion for our evening meal from our friendly hostess.

If you're ever in Farmington, the Casa Blanca and the Three Rivers Brewery are unhesitatingly recommended.

Song for the day: Little Feat – 'Willin'

We haven't been to all the places mentioned in this, perhaps the ultimate truck driving song. But we're just a bit north of Tucumcari NM today and we'll be passing close to Tehachapi CA in a few days' time. And we've certainly been warped by the rain and driven by the snow, at points along the way. Anyway, Little Feat are probably my favourite band of all time – certainly the best live band I've seen – so any excuse to include them is a good excuse.

Day 27 - TOUGH PEOPLE IN A TOUGH LAND

Farmington NM → Mexican Hat UT

After completing the New Mexico North scenic route, we embarked on the Monument Valley Meander chapter of our trusty guide. Which started with the Four Corners Monument - the point where the states of New Mexico, Arizona, Colorado and Utah intersect - and led on to scenery of a very different kind.

The Monument was a pretty bleak spot, especially on a day that started grey and very windy. Over the years there has been protracted debate about the accuracy of the surveys that placed it here. It's hard to imagine why anyone would bother to argue about the ownership of a few yards of such brutally unwelcoming, unproductive land. Until, that is, they discover oil or other mineral wealth beneath it.

The place wasn't busy, but we still had to hang about before taking our photos at the precise point of conjunction. This is marked by a bronze disc set in granite, surrounded by the seals and flags of the four states, along with the flags of the Navajo and Ute nations and the United States. Common practice is to arrange yourself in shot, either on your back or on all fours or in some other way, so you have a limb in each quadrant. Going through all the positional permutations was taking some time for each poser. For a significant percentage of them either age or bulk, or both, meant the struggle to get up again was extending the process even further. This spectacle did provide entertainment while we waited our turn, though.

Once we'd managed to do the necessary, we took a tour of the native craft stalls that ran around all four sides of the plaza. As we'd found at Taos Pueblo, the Native American stallholders were remarkably unassertive, so we were able to do this at leisure and take advantage of shelter from the chilly blast, which the stalls also provided. They sold a wide range of stuff, from high end jewellery and pottery, to t-shirts and cheap souvenirs. Some of the work was beautiful and we came away with one of the sand paintings, along with a quite lengthy description of the technique involved, shared by the artist himself.

In a bit of a state. Or rather, in bits of four states.

From the Monument we quickly crossed a sliver of Colorado before entering Utah. On paper all the land in this corner of the state belongs to the Navajo Nation, as part of the largest Native American reservation in the country - over 25,000 square miles. In practice, it belongs to Mother Nature. And she's not encouraging visitors. The US government weren't being generous when they gave it to the tribe.

For most of the day the extraordinary landscape consisted of red rock. In the form of sheer cliffs, precipitous chasms and huge outcrops, formed by the elements into a multitude of strange shapes. Travel away from the road, in any direction and by any means, would have been difficult and probably dangerous. Of life, either botanical or zoological, there was little or no sign.

In mid-afternoon the San Juan river, which had been following roughly the same course as the road, but invisibly at the bottom of deep gorges, suddenly emerged into a narrow valley of abundant greenery. We stopped at the town of Bluff, lured by a photo opportunity at the towering Navajo Twins sandstone rock formation, an unexpectedly nice cafe and a 'trading post', selling jewellery, woven baskets and other genuine Navajo crafts at stratospheric prices. $1735 for a pot that's only a few inches tall? $900 for a small rug? We swallowed hard and went to the café for a late lunch.

Weird rocks and crazy prices in Bluff.

As so often, when we see shops such as this in tourist destinations around the world, we wondered how their business model works. Even quite small places, tucked away down side streets on Mediterranean islands or standing forlornly by Third World roadsides, are usually crammed with merchandise that must be worth a small fortune – hundreds of thousands of dollars, in the case of the Bluff place, given their price tags. Much of it probably never sells. It's certainly hard to imagine many people either wanting to buy most of the items on display in the stores selling mass-produced rubbish, or being able to afford them here. So is it all on sale or return? Have the owners sunk money into stock that's effectively worthless? How it's expected to result in a profitable enterprise is a bit of a mystery.

At the Bluff Fort historic site - a reconstruction of the original 19th century community, of which nothing remains - we learned the story of the band of Mormon families, who'd been dispatched by their church leaders in 1879 to colonise this unexplored area. The journey was expected to take six weeks. It actually involved six months of unimaginable hardship and challenges, through the depths of winter and what should have been impassable country, before they reached this oasis and overcame further obstacles to settle here.

The most remarkable aspect of the expedition involved what became known as The Hole In The Rock. When the party got to the Colorado River, they were looking over it from the top of a 900 feet precipice. A very steep crevice through the rocks led down to the river, but the opening was also very narrow in places – far too narrow to allow wagons through. At this point you'd think any sane persons would have turned back or looked for an alternative way to proceed. But these particular persons were religious zealots, charged with a mission to find the most direct route to the San Juan valley.

They spent weeks, widening the crevice with gunpowder and chisels, and rearranging the rocks underfoot to create a base that wagons and livestock could at least attempt to travel over. When it was deemed ready, they used two blind horses to pull the first wagon – the other horses were too nervous (too sensible, some might say) to attempt it without a demonstration that it could be done. Everyone and everything finally made it down, reportedly without serious injury. The road, if you can call it that, is still there. No-one attempts to negotiate it these days, other than on foot, and even that involves some climbing skills.

Sadly, when those resolute souls reached this apparently more welcoming spot, their trials were far from over. Nature was not inclined to be friendly. The river flooded repeatedly, destroying both homes and crops, and the settlement was eventually abandoned. The population now numbers barely 200, most of them catering for the tourist trade. But it's still the largest town for many, many miles.

As we warmed up in our hotel room in Mexican Hat (yes, a town even smaller than Bluff), after braving a day of unseasonably cool temperatures and brisk winds, we consoled ourselves with thoughts of how those early settlers must have suffered by comparison. Whatever you may think of Mormons and their beliefs, their ancestors were hardy and resourceful to an extraordinary degree. And they didn't have a hot shower and an episode of 'Frasier' to look forward to, at the end of the day.

Mexican Hat is named after a nearby rock formation. This is yet another quirk of geology, where a large rock has been left perched on top of a much smaller one. We thought it looked more like a mushroom cloud than a sombrero, but calling your town Atomic Explosion probably isn't going to boost its visitor numbers. Especially when you're in an area that was exposed to fallout from the many nuclear tests, which were recklessly conducted by the Americans during the 1950s.

As darkness started to descend, squally showers made leaving our room a less than enticing prospect. Hunger won out, though, so we donned several layers of clothing and went a few yards up the road to the Swingin Steaks restaurant, which looked to be the only game in town. 'Restaurant' turned out to be a bit of an overclaim. There were a handful of tables and chairs under a flimsy roof, which the wind was threatening to lift off, but otherwise open to the elements. And next to them a swinging metal grill (hence the name) over a fire with hunks of meat on it. The menu was limited, to put it mildly – steak with beans, steak with Texas toast, steak with salad or a combination thereof. The steaks weren't bad, if ambitiously priced, and on a balmier evening it would no doubt have been a more enjoyable experience. As it was, we couldn't eat up and get back to our room fast enough.

Song for the day: Mike Nesmith – 'Navajo Trail'

Mike Nesmith is best known for his brief tenure with The Monkees. But he was also an accomplished musician and songwriter, whose ambitions to do his own stuff were largely thwarted during his time in the Prefab Four. He went on to make a whole string of excellent, country-ish albums and his songs were covered by the likes of Linda Ronstadt and Billie Jo Spears.

Not that he needed the money – his mother, a secretary/typist, had invented liquid paper in her kitchen and he inherited a fortune.

Day 28 - INTO THE VALLEY

Monument Valley

And so to what is one of the centrepieces of this entire trip, and what must be one of the most photographed places on earth. When people visit the Sydney Opera House or the Eiffel Tower or other popular tourist locations, they'll usually take a few shots. When they come to Monument Valley they take dozens, if not hundreds.

What's particularly impressive (and 'impressive' really doesn't do it justice) is its sheer scale. Cape Town has one Table Mountain, Monument Valley has many. Folk travel thousands of miles, at great expense and inconvenience, to see a big lump of red rock rising from the earth in the middle of Australia. Here they're everywhere you look. Some have been carved by the elements into fanciful shapes – Camel Butte, Elephant Butte and Sleeping Dragon, for example – while others have cliffs, hundreds of feet high, so sheer that they could have been cut with a monstrous saw. The first white military expedition to reach the place reported that it was "as desolate and repulsive-looking a country as can be imagined". That's not how the travel brochures, or we, would describe it.

The geologists have a scientific explanation of this phenomenal piece of topography, involving rising layers of land, receding sea water and several million years of erosion. The native people tell a more elaborate tale, featuring the daughter of First Man and First Woman, known as Changing Woman. She mated with the Sun and gave birth to twins. They, along with the rest of the tribe, were threatened by terrible monsters with names such as Monster Who Kicks People Down The Cliff and Monster That Kills With Its Eyes (I once had a boss who could have been called that). The twins had to go into hiding until they were given special powers, allowing them to turn the monsters into stone. Those stone monsters were what we saw today, scattered across the Valley. The geologists' version may be the more widely accepted one, but we know which we prefer.

Another Navajo belief, which they're far less willing to talk about, as it's believed that doing so will bring misfortune, is the existence of Skinwalkers. This is every bit as creepy as it sounds. Skinwalkers are basically medicine men who've gone bad and killed a close family member. They continue to live among the tribe but, having crossed this line, they have acquired a supernatural ability to shape shift into other people or animals, in order to do further evil undetected. Because these creatures appear in the appropriate skins – coyotes, wolves etc – the Navajo won't wear hides other than sheepskin or buckskin, and even then only for ceremonies. The Skinwalkers are said to effect their transformations at night, so we made a note not to hang around in the Valley after dark, just in case there's any truth in the legend.

A 17-mile road runs around the mesas, buttes and spires that have drawn film makers to Monument Valley, since John Ford discovered it in the 1930s and turned it into what has become, for succeeding generations worldwide, a defining image of the American West. But it's a rough dirt track with some significant ups and downs. All the guide books and most of the reviews recommended paying for a tour, as we did… and were very glad we did. It not only spared our hire car some punishment and left me free to enjoy the sights. It also took us to parts of the Valley that self-guided visits can't reach.

There's a long list of different tours available: in various vehicles, by helicopter, on horseback and on foot, nearly all run by the Navajo people. They range from group tours lasting just a couple of hours, to all-day (even all-night) private affairs at considerably greater cost. We'd gone for a 3-hour 'back country' option, which would be off the main circuit for most of the way.

We got there well ahead of our tour's midday start time, so we could check out the lie of the land and grab a coffee. The lie of the land, in literal terms, means that your first sight of the Valley comes as a dramatic reveal. From the main road and the side turning that takes you through the ticket booths at the entry point, hardly any of it can be seen, as the valley floor is at a much lower level. Sight lines are further obstructed by the extensive Visitor Center and hotel block, that now run along the rim. It's only when you park up and walk to the viewing platform at one end of the buildings that the panorama, at once so familiar and so stunning, is spread out before you.

In the footsteps of Johns Ford and Wayne.

The tour vehicles in the parking lot were a mixed bunch, from full-sized, enclosed buses to much smaller, open-sided 4WD jeeps with a capacity for nine or ten. Initially, and for most of the way round, we were delighted to be in one of the latter. Doing the tour in a crowd would not have enhanced the experience. As we found at the first viewpoint, looking out onto the celebrated East and West Mittens – two of the buttes that are shaped like a pair of mittens, side by side. (Another Navajo legend, which might seem to contradict the one about the petrified monsters, has it that they fit the gigantic hands of the Gods and have been left here, awaiting their return.) This viewpoint was the first stop-off on the loop road for every vehicle leaving the Visitor Centre, so it was swarming with people trying to line up an unimpeded shot. Thankfully we turned off the main drag soon afterwards and had things pretty much to ourselves, from there on.

However, not content with leaving the surroundings to demonstrate the awesome might of Nature, the weather gods decided to have one of their more capricious days. After setting off in clear, bright conditions, a storm swept in part of the way round, bringing a very sharp burst of hard rain and icy winds, which came straight at our faces. It almost immediately turned our skin blue and the road into something that even our rugged transportation found tricky on the inclines. Although it only lasted about 20 minutes, it was uncomfortable for all the passengers and almost unbearable for Tricia. The skies soon cleared, but the road didn't.

Once the sun re-appeared, we were able to appreciate the advantages of being on a guided tour to the full. Driving ourselves, in a run-of-the-mill saloon on surfaces that would now challenge contestants in a motocross rally, would have been no fun at all. And we wouldn't have got to any of the few places where Navajo families still live. Just after the storm had left us feeling frozen, even though our guide had hastily distributed thick blankets, we were welcomed into a cosy hogan (the traditional, beehive-shaped native dwelling) to stand by a pot-belly stove and watch a demonstration of Navajo weaving. It may well be the only time in our lives, when we wish that a demonstration of weaving could last more than ten minutes. Folk in our group were asking the most asinine questions, in order to prolong our stay by the stove. Under normal circumstances I would have found this to be a source of great irritation, but here I was inwardly applauding them.

As the tour continued, we saw more extraordinary rock formations and remnants of ancient civilisation, including petroglyphs dating back a thousand years. And our guide sang a tribal song, in a natural amphitheatre whose acoustics made her sound like Whitney Houston. As we've come to expect from the native people, there was none of the usual angling for a tip at the end of the tour, but she got one anyway. She'd really earned it.

What might have befallen our car, if we hadn't taken a guided tour.

When we were returned to the Visitor Center, we dashed inside for much-needed hot drinks, before emerging into an unexpectedly balmy evening. We spent the next hour and a half taking an utterly delightful walk, along the Lee Cly Trail at the base of a mesa sitting above the rim. Who was/is Lee Cly? From what little we've been able to find out, he was born in the Valley, went on to become the longest-serving ranger in the Tribal Park and, all being well, is still with us. The trail, which we shared with birds, small creatures and the rusty remains of a vintage car and a truck (such relics keep cropping up in the most unlikely places), is a perfect way of honouring his work.

We concluded our monumental day by having dinner while watching the sun go down on the Valley, at the aptly named View Restaurant in the hotel complex. On the way back to Mexican Hat for the night, however, it poured with rain yet again. Mother Nature had no intention of letting us forget who's boss.

Song for the day: Drive By Truckers – 'Monument Valley'

I must confess, I'd never heard this before seeking inspiration for a song to suit our day in this extraordinary place. This seems to fit the bill perfectly, especially the closing lines: "Turn your back on the comforts of home, And wander round The Monument Valley alone". Part of our visit was indeed uncomfortable, but it was also unforgettable.

Day 29 - BADLANDS START TREATING US GOOD

Monument Valley → Cameron AZ

We spent the first part of the day getting the most from our Monument Valley entrance fee, which covers admission for two days, by returning to hike the four miles long Wildcat Trail around the West Mitten, one of the most iconic buttes. It's the only trail within the Tribal Park that you can venture onto without a native guide. (The Lee Cly Trail, which we did yesterday evening, is just outside its borders.)

It was an easy and enjoyable walk, although the Park authorities seemed to treat it as if it was a Himalayan expedition. There was a noticeboard filled with warnings and instructions at the start of the trail, and we had to sign in and out at the ranger post inside the Visitors Center, so they'd know we'd survived it. Mind you, we met a couple along the way who said it had been 100 degrees when they were last there. It would have been a bit harder under those conditions. Reviews on Trip Advisor, from people who have done it at the height of summer, certainly make it seem like something of an ordeal.

Between the Mittens on the Wildcat Trail.

The trail dropped down from the rim of the Valley and took us towards, and then between, the three hulks that dominate the scene from the Visitors

Center – the West and East Mittens (see yesterday's entry) and Merrick Butte, all of them close to 1000 feet in height. The latter, while not the most evocative of the Valley's offerings in shape, does have a story attached to it.

Jack Merrick was one of the soldiers charged with clearing the Navajo out of the area in the 1860s. Noticing the silver jewellery being worn by the natives they were escorting, he concluded there must be silver deposits in the Valley and returned a decade later with a partner to look for them. By this time, some of the Navajo had also returned and insisted the prospectors leave at once or be killed. Unfortunately for them, they had already found a well-stocked silver mine and couldn't resist the urge to exploit it. They never got the chance to do so, as the tribesmen made good on their threat. Merrick cooked what was to be his last meal at the foot of the butte that now bears his name and was buried there.

Given the number of people at the Visitors Center and the steady stream of vehicles on the Loop Road, we were surprised to find we had the trail almost to ourselves. In the two hours it took to complete it, with regular stops for taking in and photographing the surroundings, we passed no more than a dozen other hikers. We could have been literally following in Jack Merrick's footsteps. It seemed unlikely that much has changed in this corner of the world over the last 150 years. Or even the last 1500 years.

After saying our farewells to Monument Valley, we continued on across the Arizona corner of the huge Navajo reservation, an area known as Canyon Country. From the car it looked like a geologist's wet dream, with land of many colours and formations, but a resident's nightmare.

Not that there are many residents. In a journey of 120 miles, we went through just two windswept, godforsaken towns and passed wretched dwellings every few miles - mostly cabins or trailers, set back from the road and surrounded by knackered vehicles.

The USA may still be the richest country in the world, in terms of GDP, but as we go further west parts of it are feeling more like the Third World. The poverty looks desperate and the infrastructure is crumbling. No doubt things will pick up again by the time we reach the Pacific, but for much of the country between the east and west coasts, both urban and rural, the American Dream is in tatters.

According to quite recent figures, the richest 1% of families now hold nearly 40% of the wealth and 90% of those remaining hold less than 25%. And that differential is widening year by year. If America is ever going to be great again, in the "all men created equal"/"pursuit of happiness" sense envisioned by the founding fathers, rather than in the "fire and fury" of their military power bragged about by Trump, that surely has to be redressed.

More geological oddities – The Elephant's Feet.

We stopped to refuel in Tuba City, which we thought might get its name from the wind blowing through it. (It's actually named after Tuuvi, a Native American who – perhaps unwisely – welcomed the first settlers to arrive here.) The lea side of the gas station building was lined with dishevelled locals, who left their shelter only to beg from the customers and exhale alcohol fumes over them. As we moved on, as quickly as we could, we found ourselves running through a sandstorm that required full headlights and a big reduction in speed.

After that we were wondering what we would find in Cameron, our destination for the night. Would it be as pathetic and abandoned as its ex-prime ministerial namesake? Thankfully, as the gateway to the eastern end of the Grand Canyon National Park, it boasted the Cameron Trading Post & Lodge - a complex of tourist-friendly facilities, including a very comfortable bedroom and a decent restaurant, both nicely decorated with native artefacts.

They also had the biggest arts/crafts/souvenir shop that we've come across so far. One of Tricia's ambitions on this trip is to find a nice piece of turquoise and silver jewellery. Turquoise is her birthstone and she already has a number of bracelets, rings and necklaces making use of it, but she hoped to add to her collection with something authentically, classically Navajo.

She spent some while – some considerable while – browsing, and had almost made a buying decision, when she announced that what she really wanted was to get something from the person who'd actually made it, rather than from a mass purveyor of items which, however attractive they might be, were of questionable provenance. I did warn her that we would be leaving the Navajo Nation first thing next day, and there may not be any further shopping opportunities within it, but her mind was made up. Whatever she bought would not have the right aura, if it didn't come from the right place and the right seller. The search continues.

If you've been paying attention, you'll have noticed that the weather has been playing a more significant role in this trip than we'd expected. It's been changing, not just from day to day but from hour to hour. The whole of the way down from Monument Valley to Cameron, we could see at least three different conditions - sun, cloud and rain - in every direction. Except when visibility was obscured by the sandstorm.

When planning our trip, all the meteorological evidence pointed to May as the ideal time to enjoy good weather and an absence of extreme events, in most if not all of the parts we'd be visiting. However, as the Weather Channel has been gleefully highlighting every night, things are going awry everywhere. The northern states are still getting wintery conditions and snow. The Midwest and parts of the South are suffering massive storms and flooding. Florida and Georgia are stifling in record breaking highs.

While the West - California, Arizona, New Mexico, etc - is at least ten degrees cooler than normal.

We've avoided the worst of it so far and it hasn't had any great impact on plans or activities yet, but the forecast for the Grand Canyon over the next couple of days isn't great. We're keeping our fingers crossed. We're also keeping an eye on the longer range forecast. In a few days we're intending to leave Las Vegas following two more of the Most Scenic Drives – first heading north up Route 93, through a rich variety of Nevada's landscapes, and then going west across the desert, along what bills itself as The Loneliest Road in America, before approaching Yosemite National Park via the Tioga Pass, at an elevation of nearly 10,000 feet.

On paper that has always looked like a particularly wonderful stretch of the journey, taking us through more spectacular scenery and giving glimpses of the Old West in the small towns scattered along the way. Sadly, unless the forecast changes dramatically, we'll be seeing it under leaden skies through rain-soaked windows and wishing for layers of winter clothing that we hadn't thought it necessary to pack. Even worse, the Tioga Pass is currently snowbound and, given current conditions, unlikely to be clear any time soon. The National Parks website shows the opening dates for the Pass in recent years, which vary widely from late April to early July. An unexpected heatwave will have to show up very soon, if 2019 is going to record a day anywhere before the start of June. It looks like we'll have to devise a Plan B in the near future.

Song for the day: The Doors – 'Riders On The Storm'

Rain storms. Snow storms. Sand storms. Take your pick, we've encountered all of them at some point of the journey. But no killers on the road, thankfully. Though there's still a way to go.

Day 30 - FEELING SMALL

Cameron AZ → The Grand Canyon

From Cameron the road rose up towards the Grand Canyon National Park. We hadn't gone far when we got a preview of what was in store, at the Little Colorado River Gorge. 'Little' refers to the river, on its way to join the bigger Colorado River inside the Grand Canyon. The Gorge, three thousand feet deep, is anything but little. The main outlook point was right on the edge of the precipice and, even though it was fenced off after a fashion, was not a comfortable place for someone who is as bad with heights as I am. As soon as the obligatory photoshoot was over, I took in the view from a safer distance.

A taste of things to come – the Little Colorado River Gorge.

A collection of wooden stalls stood next to the parking area, selling the usual array of native crafts. Tricia took her time browsing but again, despite this probably being her last chance to buy direct from Navajo people within the tribal lands, she couldn't bring herself to commit to a purchase. One guy had some jewellery which caught her eye and which he claimed to have made himself, but he didn't look anything like a full-blooded Navajo and his glib patter was quite out of keeping with the conversations we've had with any of the genuinely native people we've met. Tricia wasn't convinced and I shared her doubts. She left with a heavy heart, having decided that if she couldn't have the perfect thing she'd have nothing.

Yet someone or something was watching over her. We'd barely left the Gorge when we passed another row of wooden shacks, set back slightly from the road on a dirt pull-in. At first glance they looked semi-derelict and even abandoned, so we almost drove past. A couple of vehicles were parked outside, however, and we took a chance.

Once inside, the shacks were filled with arts and crafts stalls. One in particular had a good choice of jewellery. We got talking to the young lady in charge of the place and she told us that most of the items were made by members of her family – the jewellery by her grandmother, the dream catchers and some accessories by her mother, pottery by an uncle etc. She also spoke about traditional Navajo designs, all of which have symbolic significance and most of which are less elaborate than a lot of the pieces we've seen elsewhere, with an emphasis on the harmony and balance that are at the core of Native American philosophy.

She could have been spinning us a line, of course, but something about her manner and the apparently agenda-free nature of her explanations rang true. After some deliberation, Tricia opted for a simple but elegant oval pendant, with a classic arranged 'flower' cluster of smaller stones surrounding a single central one. She departed the shop with a smile on her face.

As soon as we reached The Grand Canyon, we were greeted with a blizzard. A proper hail-in-your-face, can't-see-a-bloody-thing blizzard. We were very appreciative of the rustic stone Watchtower, standing right next to the edge at Desert View, the first outlook we came to, even if it rapidly filled up with others seeking shelter.

It was a temporary setback. After a few minutes the weather relented and the Canyon gradually revealed its wonders. At every stop on the Southern Rim, along the fifteen or so miles to the Canyon Village, we got a mixture of sunshine and clouds. Which may have been a good thing, as it meant the scenes spread out before us were constantly changing with the light.

The Canyon's reputation precedes it, big time. Yet it doesn't disappoint in the slightest. The challenge is stopping yourself from snapping photos, so you can just drink it in. This is one instance where the eye can definitely see more than a camera. Words are hopelessly inadequate in capturing the scale and majesty of the place. The river, where it can be spied from the rim, is just a tiny ribbon, more than a mile below. It seems inconceivable that, over millions of years, it could have been responsible for creating this ridiculously huge crack in the land.

Another 'wow' moment.

What's especially extraordinary is the presence, throughout the Canyon, of peaks and gorges which would be noteworthy landmarks almost anywhere else. Here, although they each have their individual names, they're simply swallowed up by the overwhelming wonder of the Canyon as a whole. The wildly over-used adjective 'awesome' is, for once, utterly appropriate. If you're in the habit of referring to a burger or your friend's new shirt as awesome, you need to recalibrate your vocabulary, ready for when you come here. Either moderate your descriptions of everyday items to more appropriate levels, or come up with a completely new word that's going to do the Canyon justice. I'll just content myself with making a couple of observations about the scene around it.

Each year, a number of people fall to their deaths in the Canyon – three in a week, during the April just gone – and it's easy to see why. At almost every viewpoint, on a day when the ground was very wet and slippery even on paved areas, we saw folk putting themselves in great peril, in search of the perfect pic. Despite numerous warning signs and the obvious risks involved, barriers were being climbed over and trails left behind, in order to pose on the very brink of dizzying drops. And once there, simply standing wasn't enough. Yoga positions, handstands and even mock falls were apparently required for an image worthy of being posted on Instagram.

Apart from the danger to themselves and the inconvenience they would be causing to the park rangers, if they fell, these thoughtless people were getting in the way of shots that others wanted to take from much safer spots. Most of the dimwits cavorting above the Canyon, and most of those on the fatality lists we saw later, were men. No doubt this tells you something about the male psyche. Tricia just nodded sagely, when I shared the statistics with her.

The second observation is more a warning. The cunning Japanese have come up with another essential travel accessory, even more irritating than the selfie stick. Thanks to the invention of the mini drone, you'll now be able to enjoy iconic sites around the world, while listening to what sounds like a horde of angry wasps and having to keep a constant eye on a mechanical flying object, swooping around not far above your head.

Lady (and gentleman) of the Canyon.

On a more positive note, at every single stopping point, we were approached by other visitors offering to take a photo of the two of us together, to commemorate the moment. We were, of course, happy to accept. And to return the favour.

Accommodation within the Canyon National Park is limited to a handful of lodges and camping grounds. We foreswore camping years ago and the lodges were booked up months in advance, so we're staying in Tusayan, just beyond the south entrance to the Park. The permanent population of the town, barely 500, is multiplied several times over by guests at the string of resort hotels that line the road. Ours was the Red Feather Lodge, which sounds delightfully characterful but was actually a completely soulless series of Eastern European style blocks, encircled by huge parking lots. It was way cheaper than any of the lodges closer to the Canyon would have been, though, the room was fine and we're only using it for showering and sleeping, so we're not complaining.

As we've found on previous road trips, the criteria for accommodation change significantly, when you're living out of a suitcase and only staying for one or two nights. Charm ranks much lower on the wish list than having room to open those cases and leave them open; facilities such as a balcony or patio to sit on are less essential than wifi that works and a power shower; service is judged by the time taken to respond to requests and/or complaints, rather than cheery chats or the dispensation of local knowledge; and any cost that goes beyond what might be considered reasonable is seen as money wasted. On that basis, the Red Feather Lodge did perfectly well, even if it fell some way short by any aesthetic measure.

Song for the day: Ozark Mountain Daredevils – 'It'll Shine When It Shines'

As their name suggests, the band don't hail from these parts. But their music is steeped in American roots and this song just feels right for the day we've experienced. Having the patience to let the power of Mother Nature take its course, and letting her reveal her wonders in her own good time, has certainly been essential to enjoying it.

Day 31 - THE BEST LAID PLANS

The Grand Canyon

The intention for today, having spent yesterday looking down on the Canyon, was to venture inside it. There are several ways of doing this. You can fly in, by helicopter or light aircraft. You can ride in, on horseback or mule. You can take to the river, on a raft or in a canoe or kayak. Or you can walk.

The air- and waterborne options were all ruled out by safety considerations (we're nowhere near as fearless as we once were). There have been no fewer than thirty helicopter crashes, in and around the Canyon, since 1980. The record for light aircraft isn't much better. Neither is the history of drownings while navigating the river. Anxiety is never a good travelling companion, so that reduced the options considerably. Riding should certainly be less life threatening, but sitting in a saddle for many hours sounds like a recipe for great discomfort, especially for inexperienced riders such as us. Which leaves Shanks's Pony – not only our favourite mode of transport but the only one that doesn't come with a heavy price tag. Our boots and walking poles were ready for another workout.

Our plan was to hike down the popular Bright Angel Trail as far as Indian Garden, which is around the halfway point of the descent to the river. From the rim, on a clear day, you can just see the small group of buildings and shelters amid a clump of trees. Toilets and fresh water are available, but you need to take your own sustenance – it's one of the very few tourist hotspots in the world that doesn't have a café and gift shop attached. The trek takes about two hours there and more like four hours back, according to received wisdom. It promised to be a wonderful day. But the moment we looked out of our bedroom window and saw several inches of snow on the car (in Arizona, in May!), we knew it was time for a rethink.

When we got up to Grand Canyon Village, at around 10, it was still snowing and the place was almost deserted, apart from folk working or already staying there. The Canyon itself was completely invisible behind a veil of cloud. So we decided to console ourselves with a leisurely breakfast at the swanky old El Tovar Hotel, perched right next to the big drop. They don't identify the source of their name, for whatever reason. Our best guess is that it comes from Don Pedro de Tovar, one of the Spanish conquistadors of the early 16th century, who led the troop that first arrived in these parts. He didn't get as far as the Canyon, however. That was reached a few weeks later, by another contingent from the same expedition.

The establishment opened in 1905 and was considered at the time to be the most elegant hotel west of the Mississippi. It's certainly an imposing structure, built from limestone and Oregon pine, and looking somewhat like an outsized Alpine chalet. Inside it's all wood panelling and flooring, stone fireplaces, Navajo rugs, plush furnishings and stuffed wildlife. Rooms start at over £400 a night, breakfast not included.

In stark contrast to the quiet of the outside world, the lobby was swarming with people dressed by North Face and Jack Wolfskin: queuing at reception, gathering round tour guides or in earnest discussion among themselves. We immediately felt as out of place as a benefits claimant at a polo match. There was an air of angst and disgruntlement hanging over everything, however, which suggested we had at least one thing we in common. We'd all had our plans for the day disrupted.

When we got to the dining room, we feared we would be in for further disappointment – breakfast service was finishing at 10.30. Mercifully the lady at the reception desk overlooked the fact that we weren't sporting upmarket, branded attire or barking into iPhones while talking to her, and graciously ushered us in. The breakfast was the treat we'd hoped it would be and while the dining room's picture window didn't give us the views we might have wished for, it did at least allow us to measure the progress of the weather and watch the occasional passers-by struggle against the elements.

We made it last as long as we could, until we were asked if we wanted lunch and took that as a polite hint to leave. We tarried for another half hour, admiring more ethnic arts and crafts in the hotel shop. (They had some jewellery which was very similar to what Tricia had bought, only about five times more expensive.) Then, once we'd torn ourselves away from the warmth of the hotel, our revised agenda took us walking along the Rim Trail, which runs through and beyond the Canyon Village.

Canyon? What canyon?

At first all this afforded was shelter from the continuing snowstorm, in the form of the beautiful Hopi House (once a native artists' collective, now an outlet for their wares) and the equally old Verkamp's Building (once the village store, run by generations of the Verkamp family right up till 2008, now home for an interesting exhibit about the development and preservation of the Canyon as a national treasure).

In terms of conservation, the Canyon is probably under more threat now than at any time since it was designated as a National Park in 1919, with all the protection that entails. In its first year, the Park welcomed fewer than 40,000 visitors. By 2018, that figure had risen to over six million. Apart from the inevitable wear and tear inflicted by that much footfall, the spending power that comes with it represents an irresistible lure to commercial interests.

Over the past decade there have been persistent attempts to get approval for massive development, in very close proximity to the Park's borders and even inside it. One proposal that's caused a particular stir is for a 'gondola' or 'tramway' running from the rim down to the point where the Colorado and Little Colorado rivers meet, a few miles east of the Canyon Village.

This would potentially carry thousands of visitors a day to the bottom of the Canyon, where elevated walkways, a food pavilion and other facilities would await them. Plans for a massive complex of hotels, shops, parking lots and an IMAX theatre at the top are also on the table.

This spot in the Canyon has particular significance for the native people and, while the plan has met with unanimous opposition from conservation groups, as you'd expect, it's also divided opinion in the tribes. On the one hand, the desecration of sacred sites is abhorred. On the other, the tribes are desperate for the income and job creation that the developments would bring to the area.

It's a dilemma that's confronted time and again around the world, in the struggles to protect dwindling wildlife numbers and to preserve the integrity of areas of natural beauty. How do you weigh those completely justified and often urgent concerns against the equally pressing needs of the local economy? Quick and easy answers are rarely available.

Oh… there it is.

We were just grateful that we were getting to see the Canyon in relative tranquillity (thanks at least in part to the inclement weather) and before any of those development plans are allowed to intrude on it. As the afternoon progressed the snow passed, the fog lifted and we were able to enjoy more stunning vistas and the sight of a group of elk, grazing in the woods next to the trail. We ended up feeling we'd got the Canyon experience, even if we hadn't been able to do everything we'd hoped for. Next time, maybe.

Song for the day: Widespread Panic – 'You Can't Always Get What You Want'

Another song that's also a Lesson For The Day. It's a Stones song, obviously. As we're in the States, however, we'll opt for this Allman Brothers-esque live version of it, by a less well known but rather wonderful indigenous band.

Day 32 - CULTURE SHOCK AHOY!

The Grand Canyon → Las Vegas

As we drove away from the Grand Canyon, a steady stream of vehicles was heading in the opposite direction under a clear blue sky. Queues at the entry stations and car parks would have been a certainty, as well as much jockeying for position at the best viewpoints, but it would have been a perfect day for that hike we hadn't been able to do.

After an hour or so we turned off into Williams, where a bit of the original Route 66 still exists and the prospect of a late breakfast beckoned. A number of old buildings have survived, most of them now turned into gift shops or eateries, so we were able to satisfy our hunger and our thirst for nostalgia at the same time.

The neighbouring table, in the traditional diner where we chose to eat, was occupied by three people – two women, who could have been mother and daughter, and a middle-aged man. He was doing virtually all of the talking, prompted by a collection of books and paperwork laid out in front of him. The women were mostly just nodding and making sounds indicating that they were in agreement, or that they were paying attention. The thrust of his argument, from what we could hear, was the importance of spreading The Gospel and the need for assistance in fulfilling that mission. I restrained the urge to lean over and suggest that the women should think for themselves and not fall for snake oil salesmanship.

Coming from a country that's become almost completely secular, at least among the White Anglo-Saxon element of the population, the role of religion in great swathes of American life feels strange, even unsettling. Most churches in the UK get congregations that wouldn't fill the local pub, unless it's for a Christmas carol service or a Harvest Festival. In the USA, on the other hand, there are not only huge numbers of well-attended local churches, but many hundreds of so-called 'megachurches', where the faithful number in their thousands.

Prior to Trump, no American politician worth his or her salt would have dreamed of running for office, without making great play of their faith.

Even Trump pays lip service to it, despite his casual disregard for what most would consider to be basic Christian tenets. In the UK, showing the same fervour would prompt suspicion or scorn. Tony Blair, for example, was a devout Catholic for many years before making it public, but kept quiet about it. Half of all Americans think the religious affiliations of their leaders is fundamental to their roles and their electability. Only 14% of Brits agree.

Our onward journey took us through another two hundred mile stretch of rocky, sandy desolation, much of it along what was once Route 66 but is now yet more of the seemingly inescapable I-40 (see previous posts). If you only know the coasts of America and the big cities in between, you have no appreciation of just how uninhabited - uninhabitable, in many places - vast areas are. This corner of Arizona has a population density of about 15 people per square mile. The equivalent figure for the UK, even allowing for remote areas of Scotland and Wales, is over 700. And Arizona is positively overcrowded compared with the northern states – Wyoming, Montana and the Dakotas. At one point, where nothing but arid scrubland went off to the far horizon in all directions, there was a homemade sign saying 'Substantial acreage available'. Good luck with that sale.

We made another brief diversion off the freeway into Kingman. The town bills itself as 'The Heart of Historic Route 66' and is one of those that get a name check in Bobby Troup's immortal song. Our reason for stopping by was far less romantic. We'd almost run out of paracetamol and ibuprofen and knew, from previous visits to the States, that you could buy great tubs of the stuff, at a fraction of the price you'd pay in Boots, from stores such as Walmart and Walgreens. Kingman has large outlets of both – the first we've had within easy reach for several days.

We stocked up with enough of each to last for a couple of years – or kill us several times over, if used unwisely – and checked out with no hint of the advisory words that you'd get if buying the much smaller amounts allowed in Boots, or most other chemists at home. Given the opioid crisis that America has been grappling with, this ready availability of less potent but still potentially harmful medications feels like another public health disaster waiting to happen. If the prescription of opioids is being limited, as it belatedly is, what are people who have become addicted or over-reliant on them going to do? There is a thriving illegal market and there are, of course, even more dangerous alternatives. But being able to stroll into your friendly neighbourhood supermarket and waltz out with enough painkillers to numb a bull elephant seems like an attractive and very convenient option. OK, you may have to swallow handfuls of the things to achieve the desired effect, but at these prices, who cares?

When we reached Las Vegas, we realised that the emptiness of the roads on most of today's journey was due to everyone, who wasn't at the Grand Canyon, coming here for Memorial Day weekend. It took an hour to drive the last couple of miles down the Strip to our hotel, and the sidewalks along the way were as jam-packed as the road.

Finding The Mirage wasn't difficult – in fact it's literally too big to miss. A hotel with over three thousand rooms is going to stand out, even in surroundings as insanely over-developed as the Las Vegas Strip. Finding a way into the parking lot was a different matter. There was no shortage of signs around the place, but none of them provided that basic information. Our first attempt resulted in us going the wrong way, up a one-way loop round the main entrance to the hotel, and being greeted with much waving of arms and parping of horns.

Once we'd got as far as checking in, we were given an immediate taste of what hospitality Vegas-style is like. On top of the not insubstantial cost of accommodation at The Mirage, we were relieved of further sums for parking and use of the internet. Then cheerfully advised that the fridge in our room could not be used for storing our own food and drink, and that any movement whatsoever of its contents would result in being charged for them, regardless of whether they were actually consumed. No coffee making facilities or complimentary water, either, so refreshment had to be sought elsewhere.

The view from our hotel room – sadly, not a mirage.

We ventured out through the labyrinth of the hotel complex and emerged into what, after unseasonable weather at Monument Valley and the Canyon, was much appreciated warmth.

The change in population density, with the accompanying rise in noise level and tempo, was less welcome after two weeks away from big cities, however, and acclimatisation was clearly going to take a while. So we stopped at the Spanish Steps and sat having drinks for an hour, soaking up the sunshine and letting the changes sink it. Sadly the Spanish Steps in question bore no resemblance to the ones in Rome but was a bar outside the Caesar's Palace hotel. We gazed upon torrents of booze being consumed rather than the cascade of ancient fountains, and leery lads playing beer pong rather than elegant Italians promenading. It was a rude welcome to Vegas, but an appropriate and, in a limited dose, mildly amusing one.

Then it was back to The Mirage for a quick bite to eat before the eagerly anticipated (by Tricia) Cirque du Soleil's 'Love', which has been running in a specially built theatre at The Mirage since 2006. From the moment we first contemplated doing this trip, tickets for the show were right at the top of Tricia's wish list. We'd seen Cirque du Soleil before, but given the place that The Beatles have always held in her heart, this particular variant had been deemed unmissable and right here is the only place to see it.

Apparently it's all you need

'Love' purports to tell the story of the group, from their births during WWII to a pinnacle of success as bungee jumpers, through the medium of hyperactive young people rushing about waving their arms and swinging from trapezes. If the narrative was incomprehensible, the staging was undeniably imaginative and spectacular. And the music was, of course, fab.

Song for the day: The Beatles – 'Good Day Sunshine'

We (or at least I) had mixed feelings about arriving in Vegas. But the significant increase in temperature, and the accompanying opportunity to sit with a cold beer in hand and without needing a coat, was more than welcome. The good feeling it promoted was the ideal set up for the evening's entertainment.

Day 33 - VIVA LAS VEGAS?

Las Vegas

After a week or so of witnessing extraordinary spectacles created by Nature, it was time to see what Man could do, given an empty expanse of land and unlimited funds to exploit it. The comparison is not favourable to Man. In fairness, it should be said that we have friends and relatives who love Vegas and can't wait to come back. After less than 24 hours, I can't wait to get out.

I don't have anything against cities per se, even though I'm a country boy at heart. I worked in the middle of London for over thirty years without any great complaint, Tricia did so for several years before becoming a full-time mum, and we continue to make regular trips there. We've also enjoyed time in many of the world's other great metropolises, not least on this journey. New York, Paris, Sydney, Cape Town, Stockholm, Edinburgh… we'll happily revisit any of them. But there's something about Las Vegas that's uniquely repellent.

It feels like a monument to all our worst instincts – greed, selfishness, dishonesty, etc – along with a coarsening of our culture, which is one area where America undoubtedly leads (or rather misleads) the world. The city bills itself as 'The Entertainment Capital of the World', with some justification. Its unofficial nicknames – such as 'Sin City' and 'Lost Wages' – echo its darker side, however. The popular saying "What happens in Vegas, stays in Vegas", sounds like a clear admission that much of what goes on here, in all areas of leisure activity, is not something you'd feel comfortable sharing with your mum or your wife or your kids.

The list of the seven deadly sins is widely known. What's less familiar is that when Pope Gregory the First compiled that list, back in the sixth century, he also identified seven virtues – Faith, Hope, Charity, Fortitude, Justice, Prudence and Temperance. Most, if not all, of the sins are enthusiastically practised in this town. The virtues would appear to be in short supply.

It's also an assault on the senses, and not in a good way. Noise, or to be more precise a combination of noises, is constant, right round the clock. Odours from passing traffic, fast food joints and the mass of humanity come together in ever-changing but rarely pleasant blends. And the range of visual stimuli, that are constantly on offer, conflict with the need to be permanently alert to the dangers of being hit by a stretch limo taking a short cut or a stag party in a rush to reach the next bar. Given the well-established link between sensory overload and mental health issues, anyone diagnosed with a disorder, or prone to stress or anxiety, should probably take their vacations somewhere more peaceful. Apparently the average length of a visit to Las Vegas is only three to four days. Whether that's because most folk can't afford to stay any longer, or because they can't bear to, we'll leave open to debate.

The name means 'The Meadows'. Which, as the city is surrounded by deserts and barren mountains, may seem even more inappropriate than Los Angeles being called 'The City of Angels'. But many, many moons ago, before Man got to work in earnest, there were spring waters and lots of wild grass in these parts. A hundred years ago, the population was barely 2000 and the city was little more than a stopping point on the Union Pacific Railway. Then came the legalisation of casinos, the relaxation of local divorce laws and the construction of the nearby Hoover Dam, all in the 1930s. Boom time was just around the corner. There are now over 600,000 residents, most of whom work in the hospitality and entertainment businesses that serve over 40 million visitors each year.

Much of that development, from the late 40s through to the 60s, was funded by the Mafia, as a convenient way of turning their ill-gotten gains into supposedly legitimate enterprises. Although corporations have slowly but surely taken control in recent times, the perception of a 'Mob town' has lingered. When added to the close association with Frank Sinatra's Rat Pack and the Elvis Presley entourage, who made the burgeoning city their playground and were instrumental in establishing it as a go-to destination, this has given Vegas a glamour and a frisson of danger, which the opening of a Mob Museum suggests the city fathers are in no rush to erase. Movies such as 'The Godfather' and the 'Ocean's' series have only served to burnish this image.

Fast forward to the 21st century and Las Vegas has become a place that taste and restraint have forgotten, in architecture, in consumption and in personal deportment. The Strip is a jumble of monstrous hotels and random replicas, from the canals of Venice and the Eiffel Tower to the glories of ancient Rome and the Statue of Liberty. While the people who throng it are, in large part (the word 'large' is used advisedly), a terrifying testament to the effects of living on burgers, fried chicken and booze. Hits on members of rival mob families may be less frequent these days, but crimes against decorum and aesthetics are being committed every few yards.

Taking liberties with Lady Liberty.

We sat for an hour in the afternoon, enjoying a much-needed cold drink, and watched a procession of meaty thighs and buttocks stuffed into hot pants (when did they make a comeback, and why?) and bulging guts overflowing the straining waistbands of XXL shorts. And those were the well-dressed visitors. If you want to walk down a crowded street wearing just a thong and a pink wig, sipping your Pina Colada from a 2ft tall plastic Eiffel Tower, this is where to come.

We're very aware that mocking our fellow tourists leaves us wide open to a charge of snobbery. Based on the Oxford English Dictionary's definition of a snob as "A person who believes that their tastes in a particular area are superior to those of other people", we have no hesitation in pleading guilty. And I guess our guilt is only compounded by referring to the OED, rather than some less exalted example of the lexicographer's craft.

We will defend to the hilt everyone's right to dress as they wish, to eat and drink whatever they like and to spend their money as they see fit, so long as they're not breaking the law or inconveniencing their fellow citizens. But we would also defend our right to question their judgement if their appearance suggests they got dressed in the dark or under the influence, their dietary habits threaten their own health and put further pressure on limited healthcare resources, or they're willing to lose hundreds of dollars on the spin of a roulette wheel, when half the world can't afford to eat properly.

We'd been told many times that Vegas is best at night. And it is, if only because some of its naffness and scruffiness is concealed once the sun moves on, to be replaced by a world of neon. But that very transformation raises questions about its resource-gobbling existence in times of changing climate and a shortage of key resources.

A notice in our hotel bathroom bragged about the establishment's environment-friendly credentials, based on their saving a bit of water by not washing towels more often than strictly necessary. Conveniently ignoring the fact that they, together with the rest of this town, probably burn up more energy in a single evening than some small countries do in a year.

The Bellagio Fountains. Vegas at its best?

Yet after spending one such evening eating first class steaks at a terrace restaurant, while looking out at the Bellagio Fountains, it was hard not to see the place in a more kindly light.

The Fountains, named after a town on Lake Como in Northern Italy, are a network of water jets, set in a pool the size of four or five football pitches, which erupt on a regular schedule up to several hundred feet, in sync with different pieces of music. At night, when they're illuminated, it's like a giant aquatic firework display. It may well be the best entertainment in town and, ironically, it's the only thing that's free – apart from the 24/7 passing show.

Song for the day: Gram Parsons – 'Ooh Las Vegas'

The song that really sums up my feelings about this town must wait till tomorrow. But for now, its toxic combination of glamour and dissolution is captured by man who shared those same divergent qualities, so presumably was well able to recognise them when he saw them.

Day 34 - DARK MAGIC

Las Vegas

There are, it appears, two distinct sides to Las Vegas. The hectic outside world, where young folk come to party. And the casinos, where their parents and grandparents come to squander their inheritance. There was very little sign of the latter demographic on the street. Our guess was that most of the oldies never leave their chosen resort hotel. Why would they need to? At The Mirage you could in eat a different restaurant and see a different show every night for a week, without setting foot outside the front doors. And if you can't go a week without some retail therapy, they've got their own shopping mall.

The casinos, in the big hotels such as The Mirage and MGM Grand, are cavernous spaces where natural light isn't allowed to intrude. They never close and once you're in the belly of the beast, it could be any time of day or night. They contain hundreds - literally hundreds - of what used to be called fruit machines or one-armed bandits in the UK, or slot machines in the USA. Ownership and usage of these machines is controlled by regulations that vary from state to state. Texas, for example, has strict anti-gaming laws and there's just one 'slot parlor' in the entire state. Nevada, by way of contrast, is the only state in the Union that imposes no limitations.

When we used to play such machines in pubs, back in the mechanical age, they were quite straightforward. You put your money in, you pulled the handle, the reels spun round and usually you lost your investment. If you did manage to win something, it was easy to see what had produced that result. With the arrival of digital technology, they've been transformed into devices of unfathomable complexity, with more buttons than the cockpit of a space capsule. Rather than putting money in for each turn, you buy credits, which can be deployed in a multitude of combinations. The possible permutations for winning seem to be even more baffling.

Not going for broke.

We watched one woman playing for several minutes, without gleaning any idea of what was going on. We bought a couple of dollars' worth of credit on what looked to be the least incomprehensible machine, just so we could say we'd had a go. Disappointingly, we didn't hit the jackpot. (The biggest ever jackpot on a slot machine in Vegas, by the way, was nearly $40,000,000. That's right, 40 MILLION dollars. No wonder players take it seriously.)

Elsewhere, stone-faced croupiers plied their trade at lines of roulette wheels and card tables, where punters slapped their chips down in grim silence. We saw one chap, who looked anything but a high roller, drop $200 on two spins of a wheel, before slinking away with an air of crushed defeat. Everyone at the tables and machines was working with robot-like efficiency and a fierce intensity. No-one seemed to be having anything resembling fun or the "swingin' time" that's promised by Elvis's paean to his home from home. We went back outside to soak up more of the sunshine.

The Mirage has an impressive swimming pool area, set in a quasi-tropical garden, complete with waterfalls, a café/bar and a multitude of loungers. The word 'swimming' in that description is probably redundant. I can't remember seeing anyone actually swimming in it. Not least because hardly anyone in or around the pool didn't have a drink in their hand at all times. We were just grateful that our visit there didn't coincide with one of the pool parties, which seem to be a popular feature of life in Vegas.

From what we've seen in TV documentaries, these events revolve around filling the pool with so many people that there's barely room to move; plying them with quantities of alcohol that might be considered unwise in the early part of the day under a broiling sun; bombarding them with music consisting mostly of repetitive synthesised beats, at conversation killing volume; and occasionally giving them a liberal dousing with foam. It looks like a form of torture that should be banned under the Geneva Conventions. Needless to say, folk in their sixties are not part of the target audience for these events. Nor, we would imagine, are they at all welcome at them.

While we've been sitting on the Strip, having a drink and watching the world go by, one of the most common sights in the stream of traffic - apart from police cars and ambulances with flashing lights, trying to make progress en route to 'situations' – has been poster vans advertising the ready availability of young women, wearing even less than the average pedestrian, who would like nothing better than to come to your room to share quality time with you.

We wondered if the lady who turned up at your door would look like any of the ones on the posters and have a similar absence of clothing. And whether you could demand a refund under the American equivalent of the Trade Descriptions Act, if she didn't. Our curiosity, on both counts, would remain unsatisfied, but we did find out that the body responsible for policing consumer rights here – the Consumer Financial Protection Bureau – has (surprise, surprise) become almost completely inactive under the Trump administration. So it's just as well we didn't need to make a complaint.

The magic of Vegas.

For our final evening in town, we'd decided we should see a show that would be synonymous with The Entertainment Capital of the World, but a complete contrast to Cirque du Soleil. David Copperfield is probably the first name you'd associate with the word 'magician', even though he's arguably more an illusionist, and he's been a regular here for many years. The hype described him as a legendary entertainer and promised we would be delighted, confounded and dazzled. All very Vegas. So he got the vote and it was appropriate that he did, because his performance at the MGM reflected the yin and yang of the town. Some bits of it were, frankly, rubbish. A lengthy sequence, where he conversed pointlessly and unamusingly with an animatronic blue alien, made Keith Harris & Orville look like world class entertainment. While others, such as when he revealed a full-sized car poised in mid-air, out of nowhere, were genuine wtf moments.

In addition to watching the show, we got an unexpected opportunity to observe some of the cultural divide that the Atlantic spans. Every seat in the auditorium had a table in front of it to put drinks on – two hours clearly being far too long for Americans to go without refreshment. At the table on our right was a thirtysomething couple from Chicago. To our left, a family of Germans – Mutti and Vati with two teenagers. We got chatting to the couple, who told us they were regular visitors to Vegas and thought it was "awesome". They'd seen Mr Copperfield before and they assured us that he qualified for the same over-used adjective. The Germans each had a drink which lasted them for the duration, as did we. Our new American friends needed several refills to see them through. There's one difference right there: the compulsion to consume.

Once the performance started, the Germans applauded in the right places and exchanged looks, when something particularly remarkable happened. Again, as did we. I think I might even have heard restrained gasps when the car appeared. The American couple, on the other hand, were whooping and hollering at the least provocation. As were most of their compatriots in the audience. The genuinely stunning moments were greeted with shrieks, oh my gods and an abundance of awesomes. It wouldn't take long for such over-enthusiasm to grate on European sensibilities. Living with it would be intolerable for us. In short bursts, however, it's quite endearing.

The MGM is almost at the opposite end of the Strip to The Mirage, giving us one last opportunity to stroll the length of it in the cool of the evening, walk off some of the calories we've been taking on board and enjoy the Bellagio Fountains again. At 11 o'clock our day was coming to a conclusion. For most of the other people out on the street, of whom there were very many, the night was obviously still young. But then, so were they. For once, we didn't envy them in the slightest. You know you're getting old when bed is more enticing than bedlam.

So we've been to Vegas, we've done it and we're glad we can say we did it. If only so our opinions on the subject will henceforth be based on experience rather than assumption. It's a Marmite kind of place. You'll either revel in all the gaudy excess and reckless over-indulgence, or you'll feel uncomfortable with it. Even repulsed by it. We're in the latter camp. It's goodbye, not au revoir.

Song for the day: Sheryl Crow – 'Leaving Las Vegas'

Sheryl didn't write this song, but she claimed it has autobiographical resonance for her. Presumably in reference to her time as a struggling musician and back-up singer, including a stint with Michael Jackson. It rang bells for me too. "I'm leaving Las Vegas and I won't be back. No, I won't be back." Damn right.

Day 35 - A CHANGE OF DIRECTION

Las Vegas → Shoshone CA

We'd forgotten it was Memorial Day until we stopped for breakfast at a diner on the outskirts of Las Vegas and found it packed with families chowing down, in remembrance of the fallen.

We were reminded again when we got to Red Rock Canyon, just outside the city, and joined the half hour queue to get into the park. It seemed that many Vegas residents, who weren't otherwise occupied with the serious business of emptying visitors' pockets, were sharing our need for a natural detox.

Once we were through the entry point and past the first couple of parking lots, however, the traffic thinned considerably and we were soon out of the car and ready to walk. The park offers twenty six trails, of varying length and difficulty. We could very happily have spent more than half a day here, but with limited time available we decided on the Keystone Thrust, one of the less ambitious options. This sounds like a pornographic silent movie but was a pleasant walk, looking up at the multi-coloured mountains and back down the valley to the now miniscule towers along The Strip.

As we put on our boots, a young couple in the car next to us were also preparing to hike. They were taking somewhat longer as they were, to use typically disrespectful Brit terminology, 'full kit wankers'. Top end boots, which looked as if they were being worn for the first time; layers of high tech apparel; a navigation device; Camelbak hydration packs – one each; day packs stuffed with nourishment, first aid equipment, sun protection, emergency shelter and heaven knows what else.

Actually they weren't wankers at all, they were a very sweet couple and we had a nice chat with them, but they could have been accused of overdoing it, unless they were planning a long and potentially hazardous trek. Which seemed unlikely when they got a little lad, about four years old, from the back seat of their station wagon. And even more unlikely, when it became clear that he was expected to be walking with them. As we finished our hike, a couple of hours later, they'd made it barely half a mile up the trail from their car. Junior was getting a piggyback from his Dad, who was a picture of frustration.

A breath of fresh air.

The visit to Red Rock was the first stage in a complete change of plans for the next few days. We'd originally intended to leave Vegas heading north, as detailed on Day 29, and then west along Route 50, the so-called Loneliest Road In America, to reach Yosemite via the Tioga Pass. But the forecast for that itinerary is continuing to indicate temperatures no better than the low 50s and plenty of rain. And the Tioga road is still closed off by snow. So we're going into California via Death Valley and the more southerly mountains, where the weather should be far more hospitable. And, of course, it'll add another iconic destination to an already lengthy list.

As soon as we drove away from the Canyon, Las Vegas became a distant memory... another world. For the next eighty miles the road ran mostly straight as an arrow across flat scrubland, encircled by mountains without visible vegetation. We saw maybe six other vehicles the whole way. It was wonderful.

We also didn't see any sign of human habitation, until just before the Nevada/California border, when we got to Pahrump. Pahrump looked as unattractive as it sounds. Fifty years ago, it was a remote community with no paved roads and no phone service. It's since grown into a sort of Vegas

Lite. A sprawl of motels, fast food restaurants and chain retail outlets, with a population of over 30,000 and attractions that consist mainly of casinos and brothels. Nevada is the only state where prostitution is legal, but it's limited to areas with a low population. Pahrump is about as close as you can get to Las Vegas without contravening those restrictions.

If you're in search of other forms of fun and games, Trip Advisor's top suggestion is the Front Sight Firearms Training Institute, where $1000 will buy you a two day beginner's course in the defensive use of a handgun or, for just $2000, you can become adept in the tactical use of a shotgun… whatever that might mean. You almost certainly won't be surprised to learn that we only stopped to fill up with petrol – this would probably be the last chance for a while to buy fuel at sensible prices, and we didn't want to venture into a desert wilderness with a half empty tank.

We're spending the night in Shoshone, just outside the Death Valley National Park, which was basking in sunshine when we arrived. At The Shoshone Inn (the only accommodation option in town), the lady on reception greeted us warmly and treated us to an enthusiastic, detailed account of the town's history. 'Town' is perhaps something of an overclaim, for a community that now numbers just 13 residents – down from 31 a decade ago. And the history only goes back to 1910, when it was established by an enterprising businessman named Ralph Jacobus Fairbanks to take advantage of a stop on the Tonopah & Tidewater Railroad, which carried borax and other minerals out of Death Valley up until the start of WWII.

At the time it consisted of a store, a gas station, a restaurant and a boarding house, some of which are there to this day. No church, surprisingly. Although Mr Fairbanks came from Mormon stock, he clearly wasn't one of their more zealous members. The town is still owned by his descendants and survives as the last outpost of civilisation, before going into or after leaving the National Park on the south side.

We asked the lady how long she'd lived in Shoshone. She looked at us as if we were mad. Of course she didn't live in Shoshone. Who would want to do that? She came in from the afore-mentioned Pahrump to do her shifts at the inn and went back as soon as she'd finished. We knew where we'd rather be, if forced to make a choice, but were too polite to tell her.

A stroll along a dusty dirt road leading out of Shoshone soon introduced us to people who do live there… two brothers of primary school age, who came racing out of their small, single storey house when they detected signs of other life. Once we got talking and they realised we had funny accents, we had trouble shaking them off. They were full of questions about where we were from, what we were doing and what we thought of their hometown. We were soon some distance from any buildings and started to wonder if we'd be suspected of attempting to lure them away, if any of the eleven remaining citizens spotted us. So we suggested that their mother might be worrying about where they were and insisted they return home. Having no idea whether there was anyone at home to miss them, this was a bit of a long shot, but it seemed to work and they reluctantly trudged back down the road, pausing only to wave us a cheery farewell.

Another legend in its own lunchtime.

We had a good dinner on the porch of the Crowbar Cafe & Saloon (the only dining option in town), despite a loud and pompous foursome at the next table, who were falling over themselves to outdo each other with the awesomeness and extravagance of their travellers' tales. Coffee by a firepit, under beautiful old salt cedar trees in the courtyard of the Inn, was infinitely more peaceful. The desert at night offered the most astounding view of stars that I've encountered since I was camping at 8000 feet in the Atlas Mountains of Morocco a few years ago. It was as if someone had thrown a bag of sugar across the sky. Tricia had never seen anything like it.

The new plan seems to be working pretty well so far.

Song for the day: P.J. Proby – 'Somewhere'

The classic from *West Side Story*, given a melodramatic, Elvis wannabe reading that would be right at home in the place we've just left. "There's a place for us, somewhere a place for us. Peace and quiet and open air wait for us (or 'os' as PJ sings it) somewhere." I couldn't have put it better myself. And what a joy to find it again.

Day 36 - INTO THE VALLEY OF DEATH

Shoshone CA → Ridgecrest CA

In the sixty miles between Shoshone and Badwater Basin, in Death Valley, we saw precisely five other cars. What must the so-called Loneliest Road In America - Highway 50, across northern Nevada, which we would have been on today if we hadn't wimped out re the weather - be like, to qualify as even lonelier than this?

We got a taste of life (or rather, the absence of life) here when we stopped off at Ashford Mill, where the scattered remains of once solid buildings are evidence that in the past the Valley has attracted people who weren't tourists. Now the ruins stand in bleak isolation. We were there for about half an hour, during which time not a single other vehicle passed by. The mill had been used to process gold from a nearby mine, which was worked on and off for three decades, starting in 1907, by Harold Ashford and his two brothers. It's reported that the mine was able to produce barely enough gold to keep them in groceries and lawsuits with rival claimants.

The story reflects a constant theme running through the history of this land, from the Spanish conquistadors' search for the treasures of the legendary Seven Cities of Cibola, through the gold rushes of the 19th century to the hordes descending on the casinos of Las Vegas: that of the irresistible lure of supposedly easy wealth. It's a dream that's usually delivered only hardship, wasted effort or disappointment (often all three), but that's never stopped the pursuit of it. The Ashfords came to this inaccessible, inhospitable spot, spent their best years toiling in baking heat and freezing cold, and for what? They at least left a small mark and get a brief mention in guide books, thanks to their mill. Most of their fellow prospectors left (if they survived to leave) with nothing but regrets.

Our solitude ended when we reached Badwater Basin (named by an early traveller whose mule refused to drink the water from a pool in the middle of the salt flats) and a parking lot full of cars and tour buses, which had come from the other, more tourist-friendly direction to score a photo opportunity. For the first time since we were in Washington, we were hearing the voices of many nations at the same time.

At 282 feet below sea level, this is the lowest point in the western hemisphere. Signs advised against walking outside after 10am, due to extreme heat. But everywhere in the States, apart from Florida and Georgia, has been cooler than normal this month, so the thermometer in the car was reading a mere 86 degrees and we were able to stroll across the crust of the flats without perishing.

Feeling hot, hot, hot at Badwater Basin.

The warning signs aren't unwarranted, however. Temperatures in Death Valley often exceed 120 degrees in the summer months. That's no weather for hiking any great distance, but folk do it anyway, especially Europeans unfamiliar with extreme desert conditions. Sometimes they even do it without adequate preparation or equipment. The rescue services get called out to assist them on a fairly regular basis and a year with no fatalities is rare. Without the cell tower, which was put up ten years ago, it would be much harder to summon help and the Valley would probably live up to its name more often. Even with that in place, phones have no reception in many areas of the National Park and GPS is a notoriously unreliable guide here, being prone to direct users off road, down impassable tracks or into chasms. To quote the relevant chapter of The Most Scenic Drives, "exploring this challenging landscape requires a healthy respect".

One group of visitors who conspicuously failed to follow that advice was a family of Germans, who were touring the States in 1996. After they were reported missing, their hired minibus was spotted abandoned on a dirt track, which was completely unsuitable for a non-4WD vehicle, in a wilderness area where public access was forbidden. Some possessions were scattered nearby, but an extensive search found no trace of the family. They were the subject of much speculation, rumour and conspiracy theory over the following years. Their remains were eventually discovered in 2009, eight miles from where they'd left the car, identifiable only by cards in a wallet that lay among the bones.

By the time we arrived at Furnace Creek, an oasis of foliage and facilities in the middle of the Valley, the mercury was up to 96 degrees. Ice cream from the store attached to the plush resort, which makes up most of Furnace Creek, and a shady porch on which to enjoy it, were much appreciated. As were the air-conditioned rest rooms at the Visitor Center.

Refreshed and restored, we continued on our way. Even without venturing too far from the tarmac road that runs through the Valley, we experienced a variety of landscapes, in addition to the prevailing stony plains and bare mountains. At Golden Canyon we hiked up through a narrow gorge where the rocks came in red, brown, yellow and green; and as we approached the village of Stovepipe Wells (so called because some early settlers stuck a stovepipe into the ground to access much-needed water) we walked across sand dunes that wouldn't have been out of place in the Sahara. We were delighted that, through force of circumstance, we hadn't missed out on coming here.

Once away from Death Valley, we came to Panamint Valley, which led on to what might be called Worse Than Death Valley (real name Searles Valley). For the first forty miles or so, crossing this part of the Mojave Desert felt like travelling through the bleaker parts of Mongolia. We half expected to see a man with a yak and a yurt, somewhere in the distance. Then we went over a pass and descended into Trona.

What does 'a small community in San Bernadino County, California, sitting on the shores of a lake surrounded by mountains' conjure up for you? Not, I'll bet, the reality of a place that's a late but surely unbeatable contender for the title of Most Wretched Town Of The Trip.

Half the buildings in Trona appeared to be in use, while the other half were abandoned and vandalised. It was difficult to tell which was which. Searles Lake is actually a dry lake, useful only as a source of salt. The area around it is also rich in borax, potash and other minerals, which is why Trona came into existence. At either end of the town were huge chemical plants for processing those minerals, great piles of which were heaped in the open air, to be spread around when the wind blows. The high school sports field was parched earth without a blade of grass.

There were certainly photo opportunities, of a macabre kind. Stopping and getting out to take them felt like it would be risky, however. The few locals we could see didn't look like the kind of folk who would wish you a nice day. So we made do with driving slowly, dropping the car window and shooting on the move. We only did that for a few moments at a time. The air stank, which is probably what you'd expect in a town named after a chemical.

Beautiful downtown Trona.

When we googled Trona later on, from the sanctuary of our hotel, the wisdom of that decision was confirmed. It seems to be a town bereft of everything but problems. In fact, it's been described as 'The Detroit of the Desert'. The population has dropped from around 7000, during its peak of activity, to barely a quarter of that size. And most of the remaining residents are only there because they can't afford to leave. Attendance at the high school has halved – they can no longer raise enough players for a football team to play on what turns out to be the only dirt field in the country. Many of the houses have either been torched, stripped of anything worth having or taken over by squatters. You can buy a property for as little as $15000, so long as you're not worried about never being able to resell it. Jobs are scarce; drug and alcohol abuse isn't. Violent crime rates are more than double the national average – and heaven knows, America isn't the safest country on the planet.

Ridgecrest, where we're spending the night, is no-one's idea of lovely. But it offers a comfortable room, a good BBQ restaurant and air you can breathe without retching. Compared to Trona, it's a paradise.

(PS – If you thought things couldn't get much worse for Trona, in the six months after we passed through it was the epicentre of not just one but two earthquakes. Whether it will be considered worthy of the funds needed for restoration must be debatable. Notre Dame it isn't.)

Song for the day: Rev Gary Davis – 'Death Don't Have No Mercy'

I'm more familiar with The Grateful Dead's version of this lugubrious ditty. But let's go back to the source for this highly appropriate soundtrack to today's journey. Death Valley isn't called that for nothing. As too many visitors, present and past, have discovered to their cost over the years.

Day 37 - BACK TO LIFE

Ridgecrest CA → Delano CA

The best experiences are often those you haven't really planned for or expected. Today was beautiful proof of that, giving us a whole series of special moments that weren't on the agenda, even after our post-Vegas change of itinerary – those moments when the universe seems to be in perfect harmony and you're suffused with a feeling of what can only be described as bliss. They're always transitory, but no less special for that.

As we left the Mojave Desert, heading west towards the Greenhorn Mountains, we had an opportunity to pay a musical homage that wasn't part of the plan. For a few miles the road was lined with hundreds of Joshua Trees. Most people will associate this distinctive plant, from a musical perspective, with a multi-platinum selling Irish band. But for me - and those of like mind - it immediately conjures up the memory of the singer/songwriter Gram Parsons, whose sad end and legendary cremation took place in his beloved Joshua Tree National Park, a couple of hundred miles south of here.

Gram was instrumental in the merging of rock and country music in the late 60s and early 70s, with The Byrds, The Flying Burrito Brothers and as a solo artist. Unfortunately his lifestyle was as unrestrained as his musical vision, and he died of a drug overdose while staying at The Joshua Tree Inn in September 1973, at the age of 26. He'd told friends that if/when he died, he wanted to be cremated in the Park and have his ashes scattered there. His family were either unaware of this request or chose to ignore it, and his body was taken to the airport in LA to be flown back to Louisiana for burial. Two of his friends, posing as undertakers in a borrowed hearse, waltzed off with the coffin, went back to the desert and turned it into an inferno with five gallons of gasoline. They were arrested a few days later and fined $750 for the theft of the coffin. The saga was later turned into a not very good film, 'Grand Theft Parsons'. Tricia was happy just to get the edited and un-fictionalised version while we took our photos.

Have I found what I'm looking for?

Apart from my fondness for Gram's music, I have a modest personal connection with his story. Emmylou Harris, my first interviewee as a music writer (see Day 14) was his partner in song for the last year of his life and has been a torch carrier for his legacy ever since. She spent most of my time with her talking about him. Also during my brief journalistic career, I met Phil Kaufman – Gram's road manager and the man who carried out his final wishes at the Joshua Tree National Park. Phil had gone on to work with Emmylou, the Stones and many others, and become known as The Road Mangler, almost certainly the most celebrated roadie ever.

After spending some time in contemplation among the trees and sending up good thoughts to Gram's spirit, we moved on and crossed over a pass into a new valley, where the foliage abruptly became far more plentiful and varied. The dwellings we saw now were comfortable ranch houses and homesteads with horses in the paddock, rather than shacks and trailers with rusting trucks in the yard. This was a place where you could live, rather than merely exist. After a couple of weeks spent in mostly bone dry and forbidding terrain, albeit seeing some stunning sights, it made a delightful change.

Things got even better when we reached Lake Isabella, a proper lake with actual water that could sparkle in the sunshine and jetties by the shore, and then went uphill again to enter the Sequoia National Forest. A hike along the Cannell Trail, just outside the charming little mountain community of Kernville, took us to upland meadows where spring flowers bloomed, birds sang and small creatures scuttled across the path. On the way back to the car we met a local lady out for her morning constitutional, who sang the praises of Kernville as the perfect place to live and advised us on where to go for coffee.

We followed her suggestion and enjoyed an iced coffee on the porch of the Big Blue Bear café, which could almost have been something out of 'The Waltons' were it not for the prices, then carried on up the narrow valley cut by the rushing Kern River, on an increasingly steep and winding road. The one thing missing from the scene along the way was the promised sequoias. We were thinking of looking for a ranger station, to make a complaint about false advertising, when we got to the head of the valley and saw a sign for the Trail of a Hundred Giants.

Feeling very small in Long Meadow Grove.

The first sequoia we came to on the trail had been dubbed The Proclamation Tree, as it was where President Bill Clinton announced the creation of the Giant Sequoia National Monument in April 2000. It was 250 feet tall, 65 feet around and some 2000 years old. It had many other, equally impressive specimens as neighbours. The very largest sequoias have all been given their own names, often taken from past presidents and other notables. Here in Long Meadow Grove, the daddy of them is Red Chief – not quite as tall as The Proclamation Tree but with an even greater girth.

You really can't comprehend the scale of these monolithic creations until you're standing next to them, giving yourself a crick in the neck by trying to see the top. Getting anywhere near all of one into a photo was impossible, even lying flat on the ground (we did try). It seemed incredible that, only a couple of hours' drive from where little or nothing can survive, we were in conditions that support the largest living things on the planet.

Almost as striking as the upright trees were The Tumbled Twins, two sequoias which had grown together side by side for many centuries and, as the name indicates, come down together in 2011. If you search for 'falling sequoias' on YouTube, you can see a brief clip of the event, captured by a German tourist before he very sensibly retired to safer ground. The trail has had to be re-routed around them. Being able to see the roots of the trees and walk the full length of them (basically the equivalent of a 100 metres running track) gives an even better appreciation of their size.

The road down from the forest to California's great central plain wound through hills that looked much like a bigger version of some green and pleasant parts of England. A timely reminder perhaps, with less than a week of our travels to go, that there's really no place like home.

The California we've been exploring over the past couple of days has been very different from what we saw on our last visit, in 2014, when we drove up the Pacific Coast Highway from LA to Mendocino. And even less like the California that captured my imagination as a teenager – the golden beaches and golden hair conjured up by The Beach Boys, and then the alternative lifestyles and ways of thinking coming out of San Francisco and Laurel Canyon.

The landscapes, whether arid or verdant, have been rugged and very lightly populated. There's been little sign of the opportunity or prosperity, which have made California a promised land for generations of Americans. It may well have the fifth largest economy in the world, with only the USA, China, Japan and Germany boasting a bigger GDP, but that wealth isn't being generated in the parts we've just been visiting. The people here are either those who've made their pile elsewhere and can afford to relocate to somewhere like Kernville, in search of tranquillity and beauty, or those who've been by-passed by the American Dream and can't afford to be anywhere other than somewhere like Trona.

But surely that was one of the purposes of this trip: to spend at least some of the time away from the usual tourist hotspots, see a complete cross-section of the country and experience it warts 'n' all. It feels like we're doing that.

Song for the day: Van Morrison – 'Redwood Tree'

During the late 60s and early 70s, while he was relocated from Belfast to California, Van Morrison made a series of wonderful records, with a sense of joy and a generosity of spirit that have been harder to find in his more recent efforts. This is a lovely hymn to some of the planet's most extraordinary inhabitants.

Day 38 - A JOURNEY OF TWO HALVES

Delano CA → Buck Meadows CA

Today was spent getting up to Yosemite, ready for a day in the valley tomorrow.

The first half was a straight one hundred mile shot up Hwy 99, most of it through the citrus orchards and vineyards that cover much of central California. It's no wonder the owners are concerned about the prospect of His Orangeness trying to throw out the immigrants who work in them. Harvesting the crops must demand whole armies of cheap labour.

The other main feature of this stretch was the profusion of oleanders planted along the central reservation, which spill over the barriers and add colour to an otherwise unchanging scene. A soundtrack of The Beach Boys and Santana's 'Caravanserai' helped the journey pass.

Carlos Santana was one of the people I interviewed during my music journalism phase. It was an encounter that confirmed the old adage about not meeting your heroes, as you'll only be disappointed. He was heavily into his phase as a disciple of the guru Sri Chinmoy at the time, and his hotel room in Bournemouth had been turned into an approximation of a temple or shrine, with drapes, candles and smelly stuff. He gave anodyne answers to all my questions, in irritating hushed tones, and I was only too glad to get out and catch up with the rest of the band, who were rampaging around the town. I got the bulk of my article from talking with a couple of them in a launderette the next morning.

But Santana has always been one of my favourite bands and 'Caravanserai' is probably their peak achievement – the last album they made before the original line-up fell apart and it became Carlos with a bunch of sidemen. If I had to pick just ten discs (vinyl or compact) to take to a desert island, that would undoubtedly be one of them.

While we're on the subject, and to fill out a largely uneventful day, here are the other nine – for this particular moment, anyway. On another day and in another mood, some of them would change. I've only allowed one per band or artist, I've deliberately gone for a diverse selection (I'd want some variety, if I was going to be stuck with just ten albums for a long period) and they're in no particular order…

The Band – The Band: Has there ever been another group that contained such a wealth of vocal, instrumental and writing talent? You might suggest The Beatles, I'd say even they couldn't match it. The Band, looking like more like members of a religious community from the 19th century than a rock group and playing music whose origins were older still, were a complete, very welcome left turn from the excesses of psychedelia at the end of the sixties. Their first album, 'Music From Big Pink', is great. This, their next one, is even better.

Blood On The Tracks – Bob Dylan: Picking just one Dylan album, from a career that's had plenty of peaks over nearly sixty years, is a tough ask. I was working in a record shop when this first came out and someone put it on. It stopped me in my tracks – if you'll excuse the pun. An extraordinary collection of songs, running the gamut from tenderness to bitterness, written in the aftermath of his break-up with his wife Sara. Relationship difficulties have given rise to a number of fine albums. This is the pick of the bunch.

The Hangman's Beautiful Daughter – The Incredible String Band: A real Marmite of a band. I won't put them on, if Tricia is around. Their idiosyncratic approach to song writing and their use of an array of exotic instruments, most of which they probably hadn't really mastered, certainly aren't for everyone. But for me they're the quintessential reflection of a time when, all too briefly, innocence and idealism seemed like a viable basis for living. And they introduced me to a musical and philosophical palette that was completely new.

Liege and Leif – Fairport Convention: Fairport could be seen as the British equivalent of The Band, delving back into the musical roots of their country and coming up with something that paid deep respect to that legacy yet also sounded completely fresh and contemporary. They'd started the process with their previous record, 'Unhalfbricking', when fiddler player Dave Swarbrick joined the band, but this is where it reached full fruition.

Ten New Songs – Leonard Cohen: As with Dylan, trimming the Cohen catalogue down to a single representation isn't easy. In fact, I'd argue that his work has maintained a more consistently high standard than any other major artist, from 'Songs of Leonard Cohen' right through to the posthumous 'Thanks For The Dance'. I've chosen this one simply because it's so deeply atmospheric. The perfect album for a winter evening by the fire or the last light of a summer's day in the garden... or sundown on a desert island.

Hejira – Joni Mitchell: This isn't the Joni album that first springs to mind for most people, or the one that gets most acclaim – that honour would probably go to 'Blue' or maybe 'The Hissing Of Summer Lawns'. But for me, this is her musical and poetic peak. The lyrics are no less personal than those on earlier albums, but they paint a more sweeping and diverse canvas, which captures a melancholy yet addictive mood. That mood is perfectly complemented by music, made with the stellar input of players such as Jaco Pastorius and Larry Carlton, which finally leaves Joni's folk roots behind and ventures into territory which, at the time, only she was exploring. If anyone ever suggests that music outside of classical or jazz is somehow less 'grown up', make them listen to this.

Wish You Were Here – Pink Floyd: Again, not the album most associated with the name. 'Dark Side' still conjures up blissful memories of dimly lit rooms full of people in an altered state, absorbing the music in reverential silence. But this is the album of theirs that I've listened to most over the years. A friend once said that anything that comes immediately after hearing a Pink Floyd record sounds a bit thin and unsatisfying. He wasn't wrong. David Gilmour (probably my favourite guitarist – a man who makes every note count) once said that this was where they worked best as a unit, before he, Nick Mason and Rick Wright became relegated to being Roger Waters' backing band for a while. He also wasn't wrong.

Burnin' – The Wailers: I couldn't be marooned on a desert island without at least one album that's soaked up the sun. In the early 70s, reggae in the

UK was the exclusive preserve of the black community and skinheads. When I brought this back to a household of long-haired folk who listened to either rock of various kinds or the dreaded jazz/rock fusion, it was greeted with disbelief and scorn. A few years later, they were all hailing Bob Marley as a god. It also summons up an eventful night at The Lyceum in London, when the 1975 live album was recorded. Tricia had her bag pinched, by one of the many bad boys running amok through the audience, but in a strange way the tension that surrounded the gig, inside and outside, only made it more special.

Dixie Chicken – Little Feat: Little Feat are, in the face of stiff competition (not least from The Wailers), the best live band I've ever seen. And their main man, Lowell George, is one of only two interviewees from my music journalism stint, who I'd happily have spent more time with on a purely personal level. The other was Gene Clark, if you're asking. This, their third album, is where they added a significant black element, to the line-up and to the music. Terrific songs, brilliantly performed, seasoned with a rich gumbo of influences.

You may notice that all but one of these albums are from the 60s and 70s. It's not that there aren't many records that I love and admire from the following decades, as well as plenty more from that era. However, this was the time when my eyes were being opened, not just to music but to the world and ways of dealing with it. Music from back then has a deep and lasting resonance for me.

Once we'd come off the highway onto rural roads and broken the journey at the very rustic but very sweet Cathey's Valley, the second half couldn't have been more different. Two hours of hairpin bends took us down the deep valley of the Merced River and up into the mountains that form the western gateway to Yosemite National Park. Tricia was relieved that our side of the road was the one furthest away from the unprotected precipices, for most of the time.

An oasis indeed, at Cathey's Valley en route to Yosemite.

Our destination was Buck Meadows Lodge, just outside the park. (All the accommodation inside it, other than campsites, was fully booked months in advance.) We arrived in good time to shake off the travel fatigue with a stroll in the woods, a dip in the pool and a cold beer in the evening sun. Tomorrow should give us more interesting stuff to report and show.

The bear would probably have loved to join me.

Song for the day: Santana – 'Every Step Of The Way'

The 'Caravanserai' album was our companion for some of the way, on one of the less memorable days of this trip. This is the concluding track, sounding as fresh today as it did when I first heard it, nearly half a century ago.

Day 39 - THE LAST OF THE BIG TIME SPECTACLES

Yosemite National Park

Expectations for Yosemite were being built up well before we got there. Pretty much everyone we've met along the way, on learning about our plans for this road trip, has waxed effusive about how beautiful/amazing/awesome it is. While the closer we've got to arriving, the more warnings we've been hearing about the volume of visitors and the need to get into the valley at crack of dawn, to avoid huge lines at the entry points and overflowing parking lots.

We were told we'd done well not to coincide our visit here with Memorial Day. Having seen the hordes heading for the Grand Canyon and partying in Las Vegas that weekend, we could only agree.

In the event, to be honest, it fell slightly short on both counts. We were up early, if not bright, because we wanted to make the most of our one day there. We drove straight past ticket booths at the park's western entrance that weren't yet manned or womanned (is that a word?), had a plentiful choice of spots to leave the car in Yosemite Village and were eating breakfast in the Half Dome Pavilion by 8.30. We certainly weren't alone, even at that hour, but there still seemed to be parking spaces available much later, if you were willing to look for them.

And as we drove out of the park at the end of the day we agreed that, while it had been lovely, it wasn't the most beautiful/amazing/awesome place we'd witnessed. Perhaps we've become jaded by the surfeit of spectacular sights and experiences during the past few weeks. Or maybe we missed the best bits of Yosemite. We saw just one small, somewhat Disneyfied section of a park that covers over 750,000 acres. The overwhelming majority of visitors, like us on this occasion, only set foot in the seven square miles of this valley, which are set up to welcome them with opportunities to eat, drink and shop, as well as an admirably efficient shuttle bus service to ferry them between different points around the loop road. If we'd been able to come in from the east, as originally planned, over the Tioga Pass - still snowbound – and had time to explore some of the more remote, wilder areas, we would have had a quite different perspective.

John Muir, the well-travelled Scot who first came here as a shepherd and went on to become known as 'The Father of National Parks', after founding the influential Sierra Club and persuading President Theodore Roosevelt to enact innovative and far-reaching conservation programmes, called Yosemite "the brightest and best of all the Lord has built". He would surely be delighted by how his work has been carried on, from Alaska to the Florida Keys. Though maybe less enamoured of the way the ecology of some areas is threatened by an excess of visitors. And no doubt absolutely horrified by The Donald's moves to slash National Parks funding and leave large areas of hitherto protected land at the mercy of commercial interests.

One big difference between what we did see on our brief visit and the Grand Canyon or Monument Valley, is that the latter two can be fully appreciated just by looking down or across. In Yosemite Valley, the really good stuff is above you and often screened by trees. Getting the best views usually requires some considerable elevation and therefore some significant effort. For example, getting a clear sight of Sentinel Fall – the second tallest waterfall in the park – was the result of well over an hour of toiling up the steep, rocky and over-populated Upper Yosemite Falls Trail. We had to ask ourselves whether it was worth the sweat.

That hike and others during the day did, however, give us a chance to observe the contrast in trail etiquette, among the league of nations flocking to this place. The Yanks are unfailingly upbeat and polite, stepping aside to allow others through, when appropriate, and always grateful when the same courtesy is afforded to them. The Brits are much the same, but with the addition of exaggerated puffing and moaning for comic effect – a sign of weakness which no self-respecting American would ever consider revealing, whether feigned or not. Other Europeans mostly plough on with a steely determination and no acknowledgement of fellow hikers. While the Chinese and Japanese will block the path for minutes at a time, lining up their selfies, completely oblivious to the queues forming around them.

A hard-earned view of Sentinel Fall.

Fortunately, Yosemite Falls itself – the highest fall in the Park – can be admired from a much lower level. In fact there's a bridge, by the pool at its base, where you can not only see it but get sprayed by it. That's if you can get on to the bridge – it's a very popular spot for photos, while haring to and fro across it, trying to dodge the water, seemed to be a highlight of the day for many of the younger visitors.

Waterfalls are a big deal in Yosemite, you won't be surprised to learn. There are many, of different sizes and formations, and the most popular hiking trails and viewpoints tend to be concentrated on them. We were very fortunate to see them , and the rampaging Merced River which they feed, in full spate, after higher than normal winter snowfall and spring rains. If you came in the summer or autumn, when the flow has dried up, you'd probably just be looking at rocks and trees. Admittedly that would be on a grand scale, but you'd be missing a major element of what makes this place special.

What we didn't see was any sign of Yosemite's much heralded abundance of wildlife. No bears, no mountain lions, no deer, no bighorn sheep, not so much as a squirrel. They probably have the good sense to keep well away from the teeming humanity and endless stream of vehicles in this corner of the park. They've got plenty of space to call their own a little further afield, where they won't be disturbed.

El Capitan. Rather you than me!

On the way out of the valley, we stopped at El Capitan, a legend among the world's rock climbers and the setting for the scariest movie Tricia's ever seen. (I won't watch it.) The Oscar-winning documentary 'Free Solo' tells the story of a guy who went up its three and a half thousand feet unaided and without ropes. As someone who isn't good with heights, I looked up at the sheer cliff face looming above me and found it impossible to imagine why anyone would even consider such a stunt. As an occasional film maker, I was in awe of the people who shot him doing it.

As for the chap who did it, I'm torn between admiration for his physical and mental strength, which must be extraordinary, and wondering what he feels for his family and friends (if he has any). Had he considered the effect on them, if he'd been unsuccessful in his attempt? Failure, in an endeavour such as this, wouldn't allow for a second chance. There are plenty of occupations and activities that involve elements of risk, but this was nothing short of suicidal. I suspect that Tricia, as a counsellor and psychotherapist, would find him an interesting study.

Talking of family and friends, we're both really looking forward to seeing ours again, after what's been our longest ever time away from home. Phone calls and Facetime are all very well, for keeping in touch, but there's no substitute for actually being with them. Especially our grandchildren, aged 3 and 1, who no doubt will have changed enormously in six weeks. Will they even remember us? We'll soon find out.

Song for the day: Neil Young – 'Natural Beauty'

Neil, like His Bobness, hasn't always been the most consistent of artists. But he has consistently been at, or near the top of my listening list. We couldn't have six weeks' worth of Songs of the Day without one of his. This feels like the time and the place.

Day 40 - LET'S GO TO SAN FRANCISCO

Yosemite → San Francisco

Woke up, fell out of bed, saw a bear across the road - a proper big brown bear, not like the smaller black specimens we met in the Appalachians. He/she mooched around for a bit before disappearing into the woods, when other onlookers started shrieking with excitement, as young folk seem wont to do these days. (I later discovered that this would have been a black bear, despite its colouring. There are no brown or grizzly bears left in the Yosemite area – the last one was shot nearly a hundred years ago. But this one was definitely way bigger than those we'd seen a few weeks before. And it wasn't black.)

Tricia was still asleep, after a long day in Yosemite, so she missed it. But she was at least awake for our last breakfast in peaceful, rural surroundings, in the picturesque little town of Groveland. The community sprang up during the Sierra Nevada gold rush in the early 1850s, when it was known as Garrotte, due to its use of a large oak as a hanging tree. It then became Big Oak Flat (whether that's a reference to the same oak, I don't know), before settling on its current name in 1862.

A last taste of country livin'.

The Iron Door Saloon, which claims to be the oldest continually used hostelry in California, was built ten years earlier. It offered walls and ceilings full of interesting artifacts – including old photos, posters, hunters' trophies and stray bullet holes – as well as a good breakfast.

Once refreshed, we set off on the 200 miles to San Francisco, the final stop on our long and winding road. Firstly down from the mountains, past a glistening lake with weekend boaters out in force, then through rolling farm country and more huge orchards, and eventually into the tangle of freeways that surround the cities of the Bay Area.

The last couple of hours of our coast-to-coast trek were, to be honest, pretty horrible. A brutal return to the reality of 21st century urban America. For thousands of miles we've been travelling on roads which, even in cities such as Nashville and Memphis, have been easy to navigate and have allowed for enjoyment of the passing scene. Now attention had to be fully focused on the high speed antics of the fellow road users swarming around us and on instructions being barked out by the satnav at regular intervals. Not that there was anything worth looking at on either side of the freeways.

By the time we reached San Francisco proper, speed was no longer a concern, as we crawled from one street junction to another. It wasn't even rush hour, but it sure felt like it after weeks of leisurely cruising.

On a more positive note, I must give a vote of thanks for the condition of virtually all the roads we've been on. Even the smallest county backroads have been really well maintained. The pot holes and uneven surfaces that are a constant threat at home seem to be unheard of here, once you're outside of New York. Signage is good too. You never have to travel far without a reminder of which road you're on or where you're headed.

Having previously been to San Francisco on just two very fleeting visits - once when stopping off to do an interview for the Gene Clark documentary in 2011, and again when driving over the Golden Gate Bridge, following the Pacific Coast Highway up to Mendocino in 2014 - I had no appreciation of how ridiculously hilly this city is.

After dropping off the luggage at our hotel near Fisherman's Wharf, we had to return the hire car to the centre of town. This was only a couple of miles away, as the crow flies, but the direct route took us up and down a street with several inclines like the hairiest rollercoaster you've ever been on. If you remember the car chase scene in 'Bullitt', that's the street. We weren't driving at anything like the same speed as Steve McQueen, but those two miles still used up 13 miles worth of petrol, according to the indicator on the dashboard. I was trying to leave the tank as empty as possible, at the end of the journey, and was starting to worry I'd misjudged it. We must have been almost running on fumes by the time we rolled into the hire company garage.

Handing the car back took a little longer than usual, as all the paperwork for our rental had been left in the vehicle we'd originally been given, back in Washington (see Day 7). Some detailed explanation and a phone call to Washington were required, before we were signed off and free to go. We then walked back to the hotel via Chinatown and the Embarcadero along the seafront. A less direct but far less exhausting route. We'll be making full use of the city's tram and bus services while we're here.

And a return to city life.

Other than that, first impressions were mixed. After starting the day in glorious sunshine and with the thermometer in the mid 80s, Frisco was overcast and quite chilly. No sign of summertime or love-ins. And no-one we saw was wearing flowers in their hair. The guy on the front desk at our hotel told us that, like New York, the city has its own micro climate. Apparently this is due to it being built on a quite narrow strip of land between the Pacific Ocean and the large bay, with a lot of variation in height. It's not unusual to get wind, fog and rain that's out of keeping with the rest of California's sunny image, and the weather can change quite quickly and often during the day.

We also got a first sight of San Francisco's desperate homelessness problem. On every street we saw bedraggled figures, carrying their worldly possessions in a bin liner or pushing them in a shopping trolley, slumped in doorways or begging from passers-by. Many of them were not just destitute, but clearly suffering from serious mental health issues or drug and alcohol abuse. By the time we got to Fisherman's Wharf, we were zigzagging across the road to avoid being accosted by them. It was reminiscent of what I'd seen in New York, during the dark days of the early eighties. Only here the numbers looked to be even greater and, in a city I've always associated with peace, love and understanding, their presence was even more shocking.

Ironically, and tragically, it seems to be a direct product of the city's success as the epicentre of the digital revolution. The large influx of tech workers into the Bay Area has raised demand for accommodation way beyond the scope of the available housing stock to meet it. There's a strict limit on the ability to increase that stock, due to lack of space and restrictive building regulations. So the cost, of both sales and rentals, has shot up. Residents who aren't in higher paid jobs have been priced out. Those who can't leave end up sleeping rough.

Different cities in the country have different approaches to homelessness. New York puts the emphasis on providing shelter and gets accused of 'warehousing', while San Francisco has mostly opted for longer term 'real housing' solutions, without the money to actually deliver on those plans. A friend, who knows the city well, tells me that – more irony coming – the various homeless charities in the city have a vested interest in treating the symptoms rather than the causes. If there was no homelessness, there would be no need for homeless charities.

The only glimmer of hope is that the situation has become so bad, it's apparently having a noticeable effect on deterring visitors. Lots of reviews on Trip Advisor mention it, and some big conventions and corporate gatherings are starting to take their business elsewhere. As tourism is one of the city's biggest industries, the authorities are at last feeling obliged to up their response. The cynic in me suspects this will probably amount to little more than sweeping the distressing evidence away from downtown and the popular tourist areas, to somewhere less conspicuous. We can only hope that's not the case.

Thankfully our hotel is in a quiet neighbourhood, a few blocks back from the seafront, so at least these sad sights aren't right on our doorstep. And we found a decent Indian restaurant for dinner, just around the corner. It made a welcome change from the all-American menus we've been choosing from in recent weeks and, as if we needed it, gave us another opportunity to count our many blessings.

Song for the Day: Otis Redding – '(Sittin' On) The Dock Of The Bay'

I know… you were expecting Scott McKenzie, giving friendly advice on how to visit the city. But this is a far better song, sung by a far better singer. And its melancholy tone is far better suited to the San Francisco of the 21st century. The high tide of the Summer of Love has long since rolled away.

Day 41 - LOVE AND HAIGHT

San Francisco

I'd just turned 14 in the summer of 1967. To a young chap, growing up in an English backwater and still in the formative stages of musical awakening, the sounds and stories coming out of LA and San Francisco were head-turning stuff. The vision of golden youth, getting it together in the California sun, was exotic and seductive beyond belief.

John Peel, the doyen of British radio DJs, was the conduit through which most of the new music reached my ears. Firstly on Radio London and then, after the dismantling of the pirate stations, on BBC Radio One. Another important source was Mr Pike, one of the chemistry teachers at my school, who held listening sessions during break times. It was he who introduced me to The Incredible String Band and Captain Beefheart, among others. Tricia probably wouldn't thank him for it.

As we all know, of course, the innocent West Coast idyll soon turned sour. The Woodstock Nation became the Altamont Nightmare within a matter of months. As the drugs got harder, so did the mood. For too many, the search for a new way of living led to early death. But the music survives and some of it sounds as fresh and stimulating today, as it did way back then. So our visit to San Francisco wouldn't have been complete without venturing to Haight Ashbury, the area of the city that was the epicentre of that fleeting but legendary scene.

When I studied a map, before we got here, it looked like we could quite easily walk across town to The Haight (as it's known to the locals) from our hotel. That was before we encountered the hills that lie between. Rides on one of the famous cable cars, and a less photogenic bus, were called for.

The cable car system used to be citywide. Now only three lines remain, one of which – between Mason Street and Powell – starts just a stone's throw from our hotel. Once a staple of the public transport network, the cable cars are an almost exclusive preserve of tourists these days. Waiting times to get a ride can be as long as two hours, at peak times, and we'd seen a quite lengthy queue on the previous afternoon, so we were delighted to get straight on, when we arrived at the terminal, and find prime seats.

The only way to travel, when you're in Frisco.

In some ways Haight Ashbury now looks much as it probably did, back in its heyday. The streets are still lined with handsome old houses, complete with stoops and turrets. Haight Street itself is still a run of very non-corporate boutiques, stores and cafes. Colourful murals summon up a bygone age, even if they don't date back to it. And there's no shortage of people wandering around, whose minds seem to have been altered by something.

But, of course, we were more than half a century too late to experience the real magic of the place, whatever that may have been. In fact, by the time word had spread beyond the borders of San Francisco, it was probably already too late. When George Harrison dropped by, at the height of The Haight's fame, he said "I thought it was gonna be all these groovy kinds of gypsy people with cool shops making works of art and paintings and carvings, but instead it turned out to be just a lot of bums..."

Funnily enough, one of the first things we saw after getting off the bus was a couple of bums. They were a bit saggy and they belonged to two gentlemen, both of them quite old enough to behave with greater decorum, who were strolling along Haight Street wearing nothing but silver foil wrapped around their appendages, making them look as if they were ready to be thrown on the barbie.

We took photos by the appropriate street signs and in front of the houses where Janis Joplin, The Grateful Dead and Jimi Hendrix once resided. And, in keeping with the neighbourhood ethos, we had a wholefood lunch outside one of the cafes, while I brought Tricia up to speed on why these people – and this place – mattered.

The Dead have always been a bit of a curate's egg, for me. I loved the idea of the band, as the epitome of supposedly free and easy communal living, and as frontrunners in the musical experimentation that was rife at the time. The reality was less endearing, however, at least in their early years. Their actual recorded output – all that we got to hear in the UK, until they finally came to Europe in 1972 – was patchy, to put it mildly, for the first few albums. By their own admission, they were still learning how to play together, how to write and how recording studios worked, even if they were quickly becoming a unique live proposition.

All that changed, when they steered away from noodling psychedelia to follow the 'roots rock' path pioneered by The Band, started writing proper songs and made two albums at the start of the seventies – 'Workingman's Dead' and 'American Beauty' – both of which were contenders for my desert island discs list (see Day 38).

By that time life at 710 Ashbury Street, as a magnet for freeloaders, dope dealers and the local constabulary, had become intolerable and the band had headed for the hills outside town. They stayed more or less true to their hippie ideals throughout their long and illustrious career, though, playing shows that were happenings as much as they were concerts and went on for hours (Bruce Springsteen's performances are mere cameos by comparison), and making recordings of them freely available. Sadly they also reflected the dark side of the dream, with premature deaths due to drugs and alcohol, run-ins with the law and financial naivety or misfortune that threatened their continued existence at times.

Where The Dead were living.

They're one of the very few bands that I would have loved to see live, but never did. Their visits to our side of the Atlantic were few and far between. I was supposed to be at the Bickershaw Festival in Lancashire, in May 1972, where they were headlining. However, the 'friend' who was organising things for our posse sold my ticket to someone else. He may have unwittingly done me a favour. It was one of many festivals, over the years, that were turned into an ordeal by the weather. And another friend, who did manage to get her ticket, told me "I spent the first half of the show wishing they'd play 'Dark Star' and most of the second half wishing they'd stop playing 'Dark Star'".

Following in The Dead's footsteps we strolled down to Panhandle Park, where they and other bands would play for free during the Summer of

Love while The Diggers fed the kids, who'd come here to partake of the good vibes, only to end up penniless and starving. (If you've seen the Woodstock movie, you'll have seen The Diggers in action, providing the same service for the assembled nation.)

Then on through Golden Gate Park to 2400 Fulton Street, the impressive neo-classical mansion, which was Jefferson Airplane's HQ for a while in the '60s. They paid $80k for it. It's now occupied by some sort of hip digital branding agency and is worth millions, as are the other landmark properties we saw. There's a sign of changing times, if ever there was one.

En route back to base we stopped off at The Presidio, overlooking the Golden Gate Bridge. Another of the city's parklands, this one is home to a variety of old military installations, museums, hospitals and other official buildings, and back in the day bore witness to anti-war protests rather than love-ins.

And finally on to Lombard Street, the self-proclaimed 'crookedest street in the world', with no fewer than eight hairpin bends in a single, very steep block. It's one of the most visited spots in the city, so we weren't alone in seeking photo opportunities. But it was great fun watching motorists (presumably unfamiliar with the streets of San Francisco) making ill-advised attempts to negotiate it, in vehicles that were clearly too large to do it comfortably.

Songs for the Day: The Beatles – 'All You Need Is Love' and The Mothers of Invention – 'Flower Punk'.

One song that celebrates the optimism and naivety of those far off golden days. ("Nowhere you can be, that isn't where you're meant to be.") And one that expresses the cynicism which, sadly, proved to be better founded. ("I'm going to the love-in, to sit and play my bongos in the dirt.") You need both to encompass the fullness of the San Francisco story.

Day 42 - BETWEEN THE ROCK AND A HARD PLACE

San Francisco

The last full day of our trip found us surrounded by shining sea, as we went to Alcatraz and a final encounter with the National Park Service - one of the things which is truly great about America, yet which Trumplethinskin and his philistine cohorts seem intent on diminishing.

Every aspect of the experience, from the boat trips there and back to the audio tour of the jail itself, was impeccably organised and executed. Unlike at Graceland, where we were also among hordes of other visitors, nothing felt claustrophobic or rushed. And we came away with a real sense of what life on the island must have been like. For the prisoners, and also for the guards and their families who were garrisoned there.

Going out to the island made you wonder why they needed so much security in the cell blocks and the various workshops. Getting back to the mainland without some sort of proper vessel would seem to be impossible. We were told that the tides would push you out to the open sea and certain death, at a faster speed than Michael Phelps could swim in an Olympic pool.

Nevertheless, as our visit unfolded, we were regaled with stories of escape attempts, none of which is known for certain to have succeeded. Various methods – some ingenious, some crude - were used to get out of captivity. Several ended in fatalities, of would-be escapees and of officers who had the misfortune to get in their way. A few resulted in a fleeting taste of fresh air and freedom on the rocky island's shoreline. There's no record of anyone making it across the mile or so of forbidding waters that then confronted them, although some of the men who got off the Rock and were never seen again may possibly have made it.

The attempt that seems to have come closest to verifiable success happened in July 1945. A prisoner called John Giles was doing life for robbery and murder. Despite this, he was allowed to work at the island's dock, unloading army uniforms that were delivered to the island laundry to be cleaned. Over time he managed to purloin an entire uniform in his size, which he wore one day to board the launch that brought the laundry and leave Alcatraz behind. Sadly for him the boat wasn't heading straight back to San Francisco, as he'd expected. Instead it went on to Angel Island, another island in the Bay, where the army had a disembarkation centre for soldiers returning from the war. By the time it arrived, officers on Alcatraz had realised they were one prisoner short, an alert had been raised and a welcoming committee was waiting. Everyone on board had their passes inspected and, as Giles was in possession of a poor forgery, he was soon on his way back to his cell.

You can check out any time you like, but you can never leave.

Another bid for freedom, in 1962, inspired the movie 'Escape From Alcatraz', starring Clint Eastwood. This plan was rather more elaborate, involving four men, holes made with homemade drills, false walls, decoy dummy heads to put in their beds and a raft made out of raincoats. Three of the men made it out of the jail and disappeared. They were listed as 'missing presumed drowned'. The film version of the story, naturally enough, leaves the audience to decide their fate. But fifty years later police investigators revealed that a raft may have been found on Angel Island and that three men had reportedly stolen a car nearby on the night of the escape. So maybe…

Talking of movies about Alcatraz (of which there are many), before I eventually saw 'Birdman of Alcatraz', I imagined it was about yet another escape, this time involving an attempt to fly away, Icarus style. In fact, rather unexcitingly, it's about a prisoner who kept birds. The Wikipedia entry for Robert Stroud lists his occupations as 'pimp, salesman, ornithologist'. An unusual CV, I'm sure you'll agree. 'Multiple murderer' presumably doesn't qualify as an occupation, at least not a full time one. Stroud had already spent over thirty years in prison, where he not only kept birds but became something of an expert on the subject, before being transferred to Alcatraz after contriving to manufacture alcohol in his cell. Bizarrely, given the title he's remembered by, he wasn't allowed to keep birds on the Rock, so he turned his attention to the American penal system and became an authority on that too, writing a book about the history of the system. He eventually got off the island, but only to be transferred to another prison, where he died.

The film version of Stroud's story is an archetypal Hollywood redemption saga and Burt Lancaster, in an Oscar-nominated performance, portrays him as mild mannered and hard done by. This was very different to the "extremely dangerous and menacing psychopath" that those who knew him remembered. In fact a fellow inmate said "He was not a sweetheart; he was a vicious killer. I think Burt Lancaster owes us all an apology". The guided tour took us to the cell on Block D, where he spent six years in solitary confinement before spending another eleven in the prison hospital. I was happy to be acquainted with the story, but even happier not to meet the man.

We also heard about a considerably more uplifting event on Alcatraz, after the prison had been decommissioned. In 1964 a small group of Native American activists briefly occupied the island and tried to claim it for their tribe, under an old treaty that gave Indians rights to unused federal land. In November 1969 a much larger group returned and this time stayed for nineteen months, swelling in numbers to several hundred and establishing a kitchen, a clinic, schooling for the children and, perhaps most importantly, a PR department to promote their campaign for Native American rights. Supplies and celebrity visitors poured in, to support the occupation.

As we've seen elsewhere in San Francisco, however, less idealistic elements also started arriving and polluted the purity of the original aims. Scroungers, drugs and internal power struggles saw the population of the island shrink dramatically, until the authorities were able to move in and clear out the stragglers. Nevertheless, the attention they'd drawn to the cause inspired other actions elsewhere, all of which led to the changes in Native American fortunes (albeit very belated and relatively modest) that we'd learned about at the Smithsonian in Washington (see Day 5) and the Taos Pueblo (see Day 25).

The best telling of these tales came from a volunteer ranger, who could have been a stand-up comedian in an earlier life. Having witnessed an equally compelling performance by one of his colleagues, at the Abe Lincoln assassination site in Washington, we started to believe that the National Parks Service must have some sort of audition process for these guys. The National Trust back home should take note. I couldn't count the hours I've spent in their properties, trying to disengage myself from rambling old duffers, intent on draining history of any life or interest, without causing offence.

So near and yet so far.

The return journey offered fine views of San Francisco, which must have been a kind of torture for the island's inmates – a constant reminder of the life and the freedom they had lost.

Our intention, for our last dinner of the trip, was to eat al fresco while watching the sun setting over the Pacific. San Francisco's temperamental weather had other ideas. There was some sunshine and it wasn't raining, but a stiff breeze blowing off the ocean put the mockers on Plan A. Instead we found a place that gave elevated views over Fisherman's Wharf and the sea beyond, while also providing shelter from the gale and excellent burgers, to end on an all-American culinary note.

In a way it felt like going full circle, back to our very first meal in Central Park. Once again we were able to watch a cross-section of people passing by. Visitors from all nations, locals of all stations going about their business and, sadly, a significant number of 'residents' with nowhere to go and nothing to do. There's much about this country that we'll remember with great fondness. The apparent abandonment of so many of its citizens to the vagaries of fortune won't be among those good memories.

Song for the Day: The Blues Brothers – 'Jailhouse Rock'

The Elvis version would be the obvious choice for this obvious choice. But we've already communed with the King, at every stage of his reign. So we'll have this one, performed by another premature drug casualty.

Day 43 – HOMEWARD BOUND

San Francisco → Rickmansworth

As our flight back to London wouldn't be taking off till early evening, we still had a few hours to say farewell to San Francisco, after packing our bags and leaving them in safe storage at our hotel. It's been one of the more interesting places offering us sanctuary over the past six weeks. Originally established as accommodation for workers, who were helping to rebuild the city after the great earthquake of 1906, it has kept much of its original character. Unfortunately it's also kept its original dimensions and facilities. Even the most spacious rooms are cramped, while bathrooms and toilets are all communal. It has definitely felt more like a hostel than a hotel.

Ready to move on.

On the plus side, however, the San Remo is in a great location close to Fisherman's Wharf. And while walking along the picturesque little street that runs along the side of it, we came across a huge garage space filled with an extraordinary array of vintage cars and trucks. As we stopped to admire them, a guy with an oily rag in his hand appeared and invited us in for a closer look. He then proceeded to give us a guided tour, telling us how the owner of the hotel had amassed the collection and detailing the movies and TV shows that the various vehicles had appeared in.

Our first priority today, on leaving the hotel, was to get some exercise, since the latter half of the day would be spent sitting down in cramped conditions. So we decided to head up to Coit Tower, a fine art deco edifice perched on top of Telegraph Hill, which we'd seen from a distance at several points around the city. It was only about a mile away, but up a very steep incline, so it promised a good workout for our legs and lungs, as well as outstanding views.

Getting there was a clear demonstration of the beneficial effects of all the walking we've done, on urban streets and rural pathways. A climb that would have left us gasping and aching a few weeks earlier was accomplished with no great effort, leaving us fully able to appreciate the magnificent panoramas around the city and across the Bay. From here, Alcatraz looked to be within quite easy reach of the shore. Having been out there, we knew it wasn't.

Coit Tower is named after Lillie Hitchcock Coit, a wealthy and somewhat eccentric local lady, otherwise known as 'Firebelle Lil' due to her interest in firemen (make of that what you will). She left a substantial bequest to the city when she died in 1929, specifying that it should be used "in an appropriate manner for the purpose of adding to the beauty of the city which I have always loved". The 210 feet tall tower, surrounded by a small park, is the result. It's certainly an attractive addition to San Francisco's landmarks and, as it's dedicated to the firemen who died fighting the great fires that almost destroyed the city on several occasions, it also seems an appropriate commemoration of Firebelle Lil.

Back at sea level an unhurried lunch, sitting in the sunshine outside a small neighbourhood deli, gave us a chance to review our trip and compare notes. We were in agreement that it had been everything we'd hoped for, and more, although we differed a bit on what we considered to be the highlights.

Tricia, to my alarm, remembered Las Vegas with much greater fondness than it deserved. I fear she was allowing Beatles music and hot weather – both guaranteed vote winners in her book – to obscure a clear view of the town's horrors. I'll have to play the 'been there, done that' card, should the idea of a return visit ever come up in any future conversations about holiday planning.

She also looked back on Monument Valley with different eyes. While mention of the name, for me, conjures up an extraordinary landscape bathed in gorgeous evening light, her first thought was of sitting on the tour vehicle, huddled in a Navajo blanket and a plastic poncho, fearing she would freeze to death as a blizzard briefly raged.

While we finished our drinks, we each made a list of our top three experiences. Tricia's, in no particular order, were:

1. Stepping back seventy years or more to get a glimpse of life on historic Route 66 through Oklahoma and Texas, as we stayed in surviving motels, ate in surviving cafes and restaurants, and visited places full of memories and memorabilia.
2. Seeing the Grand Canyon show off its splendours in a year's worth of different weather conditions, over just two days. Particularly seeing it covered in snow, which is not how most visitors get to witness it.
3. Despite the earlier discomfort during our tour of Monument Valley, our evening walk along the Lee Cly Trail was blissful – just the two of us, in perfect conditions and perfect tranquillity. With the mesas and buttes of the Valley providing the most stunning of backdrops.

And for me, also in no particular order:

1. The Time Jumpers gig in Nashville – great musicians in a great venue with good company. Exactly what I'd hoped we would find in Music City USA. Our evening at The Ryman was an ambition fulfilled. This one was less planned and less anticipated but even better.

2. The afternoon when we hiked the delightful Cannell Trail, accompanied only by wildlife, and then walked among living giants in the Sequoia National Forest. The kind of moments in the kind of places where you feel the universe is smiling on you.
3. Sitting on the porch of our chalet in the Blue Ridge Mountains of Virginia (cue for a song), watching the sun set over the Shenandoah Valley. After a week in the hustle and bustle of New York and Washington, this was when I thought the trip had really begun and was sure it was going to be great.

How we'd like to remember San Francisco.

We'd booked a ride on a shuttle service, picking us up from our hotel, to get to the airport. It was a lot cheaper than a taxi and a lot easier than trying to negotiate several changes of public transport with suitcases, and it worked exactly as advertised. The roads out of town were congested and far from lovely, though. Away from the parts visited by tourists, San Francisco, from what we saw, was run down, scruffy and a prime example of urban blight. Many more homeless people and rudimentary shelters for them lined the route. We didn't leave our hearts there.

Once at the airport, the uniqueness of our journey was over, to be replaced by the all-too-familiar rigmarole of international travel – queuing, cups of inferior coffee, some more queuing and eleven hours of unappetising food and intermittent sleep – before arriving back at Heathrow and the very welcome sight of our son Jack, waiting to whisk us home.

Song for the Day: Peter Cook & Dudley Moore – 'Goodbye-ee'.

The songs so far have, quite rightly, been mostly American. Reflecting the musics and the attitudes of this great land and its people. But as we bid farewell and head home, let's re-acclimatise with a ditty that could only have come from dear old Blighty. The love of sheer silliness and the inclination to mask real emotion with throwaway humour would be alien to most Americans, but it is at the heart of our national character.

Day 44 - IT'S ALL OVER NOW

Back home

We drove 4721 miles and took over a million steps across nineteen states. The average American sees just twelve in a whole lifetime, apparently.

We travelled under spacious skies, through purple mountains' majesties and across fruited plains.

We stayed in some of the biggest cities, and in towns that were little more than a motel and a gas station. (The smallest was Shoshone, on the edge of Death Valley - pop.13.)

We saw a Broadway show, a couple of Las Vegas extravaganzas and a gig at the Ryman, as well as numerous bar bands and street performers of varying quality along the way.

We went to places where famous citizens, from Abe Lincoln to Elvis, as well as characters of less notoriety but still of real interest, had lived and died.

We watched the world go by on Times Square, Beale Street, the Vegas Strip and Fisherman's Wharf.

We hiked in forests, mountains and deserts from the Appalachians to Yosemite Valley. And witnessed the wonders of Monument Valley and The Grand Canyon.

We ate the finest BBQ ribs in the land, the best burgers in Memphis, and 'famous' everything from fish & chips to French toast.

And we met a whole host of lovely, friendly people.

Did we see America? We certainly experienced a big cross section of it. Were we impressed? Pretty much every day. Several times in one day, on many occasions.

But would we want to live there? Hell, no. It's scarred by obscene riches and obscene poverty, while the wealthy minority and corporations wield an influence which is eroding the democracy and principles on which the country was founded. It seems to be in a spiral of reckless consumption, which is threatening the health of individuals, of society and of the planet. Many of the most lovely places are too remote for everyday existence, unless you crave complete solitude. And their TV is absolute shit - with conspicuous exceptions, which we get to see at home anyway.

They say "America - love it or leave it". We've been able to do both. And after six weeks of living in each other's pockets 24/7, we're still talking and still laughing together. Which can't be bad. We're already looking forward to the next road trip.

Song for the Day: Simon & Garfunkel – 'America'

We didn't do it on Greyhound buses or by hitchhiking. (I don't think anyone hitchhikes in America these days – we certainly saw no sign of it.) And we didn't count cars on the New Jersey Turnpike (see Day 5). But we did marry our fortunes together and go looking for America. For better and for worse, I think we found it.

THE SOUNDTRACK

Lenny Kravitz – 'Fly Away' from '5' (1998)

Art Garfunkel - 'A Heart In New York' from 'Scissors Cut' (1981)

Lou Reed - 'Perfect Day' from 'Transformer' (1972)

Bruce Springsteen - 'My City Of Ruins' from 'The Rising' (2002)

Bob Dylan - 'A Hard Rain's Gonna Fall' from 'Freewheelin'' (1963)

Green Day - 'American Idiot' from 'American Idiot' (2004)

Marvin Gaye - 'Abraham, Martin & John' from 'That's The Way Love Is' (1970)

The Carter Family - 'Mid The Green Fields Of Virginia' First released as a 78rpm in 1932

Mary Chapin Carpenter - 'Good Night America' from 'Between Here And Gone' (2004)

John Otway & Wild Willy Barrett - 'Misty Mountain' from 'John Otway & Wild Willy Barrett' (1977)

The Dillards - 'Old Man At The Mill' from 'Copperfields' (1970)

Dwight Yoakam – 'Waterfall' from '3 Pears' (2012)

Dolly Parton - 'My Tennessee Mountain Home' from 'My Tennessee Mountain Home' (1973)

Steve Earle - 'Guitar Town' from 'Guitar Town' (1986)

The Lovin' Spoonful - 'Nashville Cats' from 'Hums Of The Lovin' Spoonful' (1966)

ZZ Top - 'My Head's In Mississippi' from 'Recycler' (1990)

Elvis Presley - 'Don't Cry Daddy' from 'Elvis In Memphis' (1998 re-issue)

Gillian Welch - 'Elvis Presley Blues' from 'Time (The Revelator)' (2001)

Robert Johnson - 'Cross Road Blues' First released as a 78rpm in 1937

Charley Patton - 'High Water Everywhere' First released as a 78rpm in 1929

Levon Helm - 'Wide River To Cross' from 'Dirt Farmer' (2007)

Vince Gill - 'The Old Lucky Diamond Motel' from 'Guitar Slinger' (2011)

Bruce Springsteen - 'The Ghost Of Tom Joad' from 'The Ghost Of Tom Joad' (1995)

John Mellancamp - 'Small Town' from 'Scarecrow' (1985)

Waylon Jennings - 'Taos, New Mexico' from 'Love Of The Common People' (1967)

Woody Guthrie - 'This Land Is Your Land' from 'This Land Is My Land – American Work Songs' (1951)

Little Feat - 'Willin'' from 'Sailin' Shoes' (1972)

Mike Nesmith - 'Navajo Trail' from 'From A Radio Engine To The Photon Wing' (1977)

Drive By Truckers - 'Monument Valley' from 'Brighter Than Creation's Dark' (2008)

The Doors - 'Riders On The Storm' from 'L.A, Woman' (1971)

Ozark Mountain Daredevils – 'It'll Shine When It Shines' from 'It'll Shine When It Shines' (1974)

Widespread Panic - 'You Can't Always Get What You Want' Multiple live versions

The Beatles - 'Good Day Sunshine' from 'Revolver' (1966)

Gram Parsons - 'Ooh Las Vegas' from 'Grievous Angel' (1974)

Sheryl Crow - 'Leaving Las Vegas' from 'Tuesday Night Music Club' (1993)

P.J. Proby - 'Somewhere' from 'Somewhere' (1965)

Rev. Gary Davis - 'Death Don't Have No Mercy' from 'Harlem Street Singer' (1960)

Van Morrison - 'Redwood Tree' from 'St Dominic's Preview' (1972)

Santana - 'Every Step Of The Way' from 'Caravanserai' (1972)

Neil Young - 'Natural Beauty' from 'Harvest Moon' (1992)

Otis Redding - '(Sittin' On) The Dock Of The Bay' from 'The Dock Of The Bay' (1968)

The Beatles - 'All You Need Is Love' from 'Magical Mystery Tour' (1967)

The Mothers Of Invention - 'Flower Punk' from 'We're Only In It For The Money' (1968)

The Blues Brothers - 'Jailhouse Rock' from 'The Blues Brothers OST' (1986)

Peter Cook & Dudley Moore - 'Goodbye-eee' First released as a 45rpm in 1965

Simon & Garfunkel - 'America' from 'Bookends' (1968)

Printed in Great Britain
by Amazon